PRAISE FOR
THE SCIENCE OF WAR...

This is an important read for anyone concerned with the growing influence of China. Christopher MacDonald gives us an excellent reading of the classic and both puts it in its historical context and considers China's policies today in terms of its ancient strategies.
—Jamil Anderlini, Asia Editor for the *Financial Times*

Uniquely useful...a superb reading of the classic. Sun Tzu comes to us, over more than two millennia, as a manual on how to live in a complex world where intelligent strategy is essential for survival. This valuable and comprehensive edition includes both the Chinese text and the translation, along with explanations of places where the text is in doubt, or where there are several possible translations.
—Diana Lary, Professor emerita of History, University of British Columbia. Author of *The Chinese People at War* (2010) and *China's Civil War* (2015)

MacDonald has provided his readers with a masterly new translation... preceded by a thorough analysis of the work that avoids the plodding approach of many earlier writers.
—Christopher Coker, Professor of International Relations, The London School of Economics and Political Science (LSE). Author of *The Improbable War: China, the United States and the Logic of Great Power Conflict* (2015)

A serious and valuable effort to dig new meaning out of the ancient Chinese masterpiece. The author's argument that the Chinese Communist Party has adopted a Sun Tzu-tinted, Warring States-lensed approach to China's foreign relations in order to maximize its national interest is both interesting and inspiring.

—Dr. Zhang Zhexin, Research Fellow at the Shanghai Institutes for International Studies (SIIS) and Deputy Editor of *China Quarterly of International Strategic Studies*

This new translation and commentary offers an excellent resource for anyone wishing to gain insight into the 21st-century objectives of the PRC.

—Dr. Tim Summers, The Chinese University of Hong Kong and Chatham House

THE
SCIENCE OF WAR

Sun Tzu's *Art of War*
re-translated and re-considered

Christopher MacDonald

EARNSHAW
BOOKS

The Science of War

By Christopher MacDonald

ISBN-13: 978-988-8422-69-2

Cover design: Jason Wong

This book has been reset in 10pt Book Antiqua. Spellings and punctuations are left as in the original edition.

HISTORY / Asia / China

HISTORY / Military / Strategy

Political science / Security (National & International)

EB092

Published by Earnshaw Books Ltd. (Hong Kong)

In memory of Donald

and with thanks to scholars 馬嘉瑞 *and* 唐久寵

CONTENTS

LIST OF MAPS

FOREWORD
BY PROFESSOR CHRISTOPHER COKER

IN THE RUN-UP to the first Gulf War (1990-91) the US army shipped a hundred thousand books to the troops while they waited for the war to begin, among them many copies of Sun Tzu's great work. Back in the United States, the American war theorist John Boyd, who Donald Rumsfeld once called "the most influential military thinker since Sun Tzu" gave a lecture on the great Chinese master which lasted eight hours spread over two days, and involved 380 PowerPoint slides. It was Boyd who sold to the generals the winning strategy of not attacking Kuwait City in a frontal assault, but outflanking it.

In the West, however, the reputation of Sun Tzu has waxed and waned. Harlan Ulan, the military strategist who conceived the term 'Shock and Awe,' specifically cited Sun Tzu as his chief source of inspiration. But some academics have been much more sceptical. The British strategist Colin Gray famously dismissed *The Art of War* as a 'cookbook'; Thomas Rid more recently complained that the book reads at times like 'a choppy Twitter feed from 500 BC'. Even Sun Tzu's Western admirers have not always done justice to the author or his work. Take Gen Tommy Franks, the architect of the second Gulf War, who liked to boast that he could quote *The Art of War* by heart. Franks was an able tactician but a lousy strategist and it was clear as soon as the insurgency began that he had memorised a series of bullet points rather than absorbed the real lessons of Sun Tzu's book. Even in popular culture the great Chinese thinker has been treated with scant respect. Tony Soprano was advised by his therapist to read *The Art of War* – and why not, you might ask if you think it's all about deception and deceitfulness, the very qualities surely needed by a Mafia boss. The ultimate insult was the film *The Art of War*, a lacklustre movie starring Wesley Snipes which traded on the book's name and nothing else. It was followed by two direct-to-video sequels, *The Art of War 2: Betrayal* and *The Art of War 3: Retribution*.

Reading Christopher MacDonald's new translation, it is startling how current some of Sun Tzu's injunctions sound. War is a necessary evil, so wage it only when you have to and wage it quickly because the longer you fight the more likely you will be destroyed by it. It is evil, but of course not in any moral sense, in that people die, but because it disturbs the Dao, the harmony of the world. It is necessary because of the wilfulness of human beings – necessity is the one force that can make people risk their lives and justify their deaths. Necessity is the one thing to get people to kill with a good conscience. Many of my students still think of war as cutting throats and bludgeoning people over the head. But Sun Tzu asks us to treat war as a problem of intelligence. Be smart: try deception, secrecy and surprise. That's why *The Art of War* is so popular with businessmen: it is as important in the boardroom as it is in a military academy.

One reason why his advice resonates so much is that it brings contemporary conflicts to mind, especially the continuing diplomatic tussle between China and the United States. MacDonald goes to great lengths to show how the Chinese leadership seems to be fully conversant with the thinking of the most famous philosopher of war. As Henry Kissinger writes, in no other country is it conceivable that a modern leader would initiate a major national undertaking by invoking strategic principles from a millennium ago, nor that he could confidently expect his colleagues to understand the significance of his allusions. "Yet China is singular. No other country can claim so long and continuous a civilisation or such an intimate link to its ancient past and the classical principles of strategic statesmanship."

In its relations with the US, the country is going with what Sun Tzu calls *shi* - a tough word to translate since it can mean many things including power and potential but MacDonald hits the nail on the head, I think, by rendering it in his translation of the work as 'strategic dominance.'

MacDonald has provided his English-speaking readers with a masterly new translation. It is preceded by a thorough analysis of the work that avoids the plodding approach of many earlier writers. He has opted instead for something more open-ended and impressionistic. There are short chapters on such concepts as oblique/direct, empty/solid, victory and strategic dominance. He is refreshingly thorough in laying out the concepts before applying them to analyse the campaigns that help throw them into even greater relief. The relationship he establishes between his critical and historical analysis is challenging. And for all his cautious rigour, MacDonald is drawn to the human beneath the analytical categories. Cao Cao, one of the greatest generals of his or any age, is here brought to life, as are Genghis Khan's tactics which so influenced Soviet thinking in the 1920s.

Sun Tzu, he adds, produced less a theory of war than a science which offered commanders "a tool for prioritising their energies and resources during the run-up to war, along with a menu of practical methods for winning it." He is interested in exploring the many dimensions of that science, including its philosophical underpinning which continues to elude many Western strategists; the historical context of the book which escapes most of us in the West who have at best an imperfect acquaintance with Chinese history; and the way in which some of the great generals of the past intuited some of Sun Tzu's main theoretical constructs. One was Genghis Khan, another was Napoleon who we tend to think of in Clausewitzian terms, in large part because Clausewitz encouraged us to do so.

In an age of pop intellectualism and big buzzy ideas condensed into short books or tailor-made TED talks, *The Art of War* is popular because it is deceptively short. My students gravitate towards it for that reason. But the book's first readers would have been familiar with its philosophical first principles. The West needs to understand it more comprehensively as its freedom of manoeuvre and margin for error become more constrained over time. For the past twenty years, we thought we didn't need to think strategically. We set ourselves ambitious tasks such as regime change in Iraq and nation-building in Afghanistan, only to find ourselves dealing with the unforeseen consequences of our own actions. Daoism celebrates the harmony of the universe: it implores us to live in harmony with our environment (to be green); to be in harmony with society (to be sociable); and above all to be in harmony with ourselves (to be content). Discontented people are dangerous: usually they are far too ambitious. There is a famous Daoist saying: those who win five victories will meet with disaster; those who win four will be exhausted; those who win three will become warlords; those who win two will become king; and those who win one will become Emperor. This is the exact inversion of the Western obsession with defying the odds, risking all on a throw of the dice.

The marketplace of ideas may be changing fast. Cadets in military colleges no longer get their ideas just from the military classics, but from contemporary blogs, think-tank papers written by today's leading strategic thinkers and, yes, even from TED talks. And why not? No one has ownership of the truth, only a version of it. But the classics are still read because they have much to teach us.

MacDonald is a lively and engaging writer who wears his scholarship lightly. His book also benefits from first-hand experience of living in China and translating many Chinese works. His approach to *The Art of War* is measured and balanced. It's one that won't necessarily appeal to the government in China but it won't surprise it either. Sun Tzu, after all tells it as it is – and, for that matter, always has been. Which is why this 2,000-year-old writer still lives in the imagination of the world's oldest surviving civilisation, and for that reason alone should live in the imagination of the rest of us.

Christopher Coker
Professor of International Relations
The London School of Economics and Political Science

FOREWORD
BY DR. ZHANG ZHEXIN

FOR ANY AUTHOR, it is always enticing but risky to challenge established notions and, as we read in this book, traditional beliefs. To most Western readers, the *Sun-tzu* is by and large a condensed precursor two millennia ahead of Clausewitz's *On War*, highlighting sober deliberation of war and detailed stratagems for each war scenario; despite the profound military philosophy — put simply, war is costly and thus requires much more wisdom than valor — that leads through all the chapters, it has been regarded as an "art" to warfare, a guidebook on how to win a war decisively and with least casualties.

That view, the author boldly argues, undervalues the "most succinct, comprehensive and best structured *bingfa* (strategy guide) of the era... that pioneered the science of war (page 28)." For not only does the *Sun-tzu* provide "a functional compilation of tactical and strategic guidance," but also those strategies are "presented in a coherent framework of theory and grounded on familiar philosophical footings (29)." That coherence and emphasis on the strategic context of various military operations and even of war itself makes the *Sun-tzu* an earliest scientific attempt to approach war from a holistic and dispassionate perspective, rather than a "jumbled repository of aphorisms, mundane in places and mystical in others (48)." Critiquing past translations of the *Sun-tzu*, the author retranslates the masterpiece and, maybe more helpful to readers, explains why he chooses to interpret a word or phrase in ways different from

CHRISTOPHER MACDONALD

the notions commonly accepted in the past.

This is definitely a serious and valuable effort to dig new meanings out of the ancient Chinese masterpiece, and the author's argument that the Chinese Communist Party (CCP) has adopted a Sun Tzu-tinted, Warring States-lensed approach to China's foreign relations in order to maximize its national interest is both interesting and inspiring. However, it would be simplistic to draw too close a parallel between the Kingdom of Wu, to which Sun Tzu served as a military adviser, and China today.

Thanks to lasting technological advancement and globalization, the world is getting smaller and flatter, with highly intertwined interests and more balanced economic development, at least among major powers. It would be unthinkable today for any single power to "dominate" the world like Pax Britannica in the 19th century or Pax Americana for less than two decades following the end of the Cold War. In fact, even those Realists like John Mearsheimer and Joseph Nye argue that the United States has never been a true "dominator," for it has had neither the financial nor the military resources to impose formal global hegemony.

Indeed, all major powers have the ambition to lead the world by their own rule and to ultimately serve their own interests. But being a leader is different from being a dominator—the former mostly by example while the latter, by force. It is here that the author is perhaps too judgmental about the CCP's grand strategy: on one hand, he notes the stated intention of the CCP to strive for "a future world overseen, but not bullied, by a virtuous and non-hegemonic China (89)"; on the other hand, it appears he believes the China Dream proposed by Chinese President Xi Jinping in 2012 is to "re-set the hierarchy of international power back to the early 19th century," a vision of China which "dominates East

Asia and tops the global tables for wealth and influence (88)."
That risks both overestimating China's development potential
and undervaluing the China Dream.

Despite the rapid economic growth in few megacities mainly
located along the coastline, China remains the largest of the
world's developing nations, with nearly half of its population
living in rural areas and an average income per capita about 12
percent of that of Americans. As Xi Jinping said in his address to
the 19th CCP Congress on October 18, 2017, the CCP's paramount
task at least for the next decades is to lead China towards more
balanced and sustainable development so as to meet people's
growing need for a better life, and "to realize that the China
Dream requires a peaceful international environment and stable
global order."

Thus, the primary goal of the China Dream is not about
toppling the global order or dominating the world, but extending
China's peaceful rise; it is not about maximizing China's interests
at the expense of others, but seeking win-win resolutions to
international conflicts and cooperation. In other words, it has
been fully recognized by the CCP leadership that without further
integrating into the world system and helping maintain stability
of the global order, it is impossible for China to keep its pace of
development, not to say to become the next world leader. Yet
when it does grow to be a world leader by peaceful engagement
with other nations and contributing to the incremental reform of
the global order, then other nations will not worry about China's
rise any more, but may instead look to China for more global
leadership and public contributions.

That is the ultimate paradox of the China Dream. The CCP
does not necessarily regard the United States as a formidable rival
and is not necessarily scheming to win in a Warring States-type
"zero-sum struggle" as the author suggests. Rather, it will keep

seeking U.S. understanding and cooperation to maximize their shared interests and global common good. Nor does the CCP aim to avenge the "Hundred Years of National Humiliation," since, as the author agrees, it is mainly part of the CCP's patriotic education for national unity and to rally support for its leadership—a means to an end, and that end is a China strong and confident enough to be a "virtuous and non-hegemonic" leader of the international community.

To facilitate this more benign scenario, one needs to be cautious in observing contemporary China through the Warring States lens, but should give more regard to the many economic, social and cultural initiatives that China has advanced on regional and global platforms in the past few years. No king in the 4th century B.C. would have cared so much about peace and well-being of the "world under heaven."

Dr. Zhang Zhexin
Research Fellow at Shanghai Institutes for International Studies
(SIIS) Deputy Editor of *China Quarterly of International Strategic Studies*

FOREWORD
BY DR. TIM SUMMERS

WE TEND TO think of the rise of China primarily as something with which the rest of the world has to come to grips with. But is also presents strategists and leaders in Beijing with a new set of challenges of their own. How should they understand the complexities of the international environment? What analytical tools and frameworks should they use in working out how to maximise China's interests? Concepts developed in international relations and security studies in the US and elsewhere have been influential in China since the 1980s, but for many this is not satisfactory. Are these approaches suitable for understanding a country such as China, which traces its history back several thousands of years and where the nation state was only consolidated in recent memory?

Since the mid-19th century intellectuals in China have looked to non-Chinese ideas and techniques where these are useful, but tried to indigenise them in ways appropriate to the Chinese situation. This hints at a deep-rooted "will to difference", and as China's national strength has grown one consequence of this has been for Chinese strategists and scholars to look again to what they call "Chinese" history from periods before anything resembling today's China came into being. The aim of this endeavour is to find inspiration for the development of distinctly Chinese approaches to foreign and security policy. The historical resources are rich. For example, Tsinghua University international relations scholar Yan Xuetong looks to the "kingly way" (wangdao, translated by Daniel Bell as "humane authority") for a model of how an ethical - and therefore successful - ruler should behave, while Zhao Tingyang has popularised the idea that the imperial-era notion of Tianxia ("all under heaven") might provide some sort of model or system for a future world order.

Possibly the most famous historical resource for such endeavours – both in and outside China – is the book known as Sun Tzu's *Art of War*. It is this which is the subject of historical analysis and a new translation in this stimulating new book by Christopher MacDonald.

Among the arguments MacDonald makes is that the principles of this treatise were not only reflected in Mao's influential *On Guerrilla Warfare*, but that they continue to play an important role in the People's Republic of China's strategic philosophy today; that PLA officers today learn to recite Sun Tzu is *prima facie* evidence of this. And the two key principles MacDonald distills from Sun Tzu - maximising prospects of victory in war by stealthily accruing strategic advantage across the full political and military spectrum, and minimizing the risk and cost of war by aiming to achieve your aims without battle if possible (p. 85) - certainly resonate with much analysis of current Chinese strategic thinking. Under Xi Jinping, the realist competitive strategic approach which we find in Sun Tzu seems to be gaining currency, though it still sits alongside language which owes more to Confucianism or the liberal internationalist vocabulary of "win-win".

In the end, discerning the precise connection between these ideas and the development of strategy in China is of course a challenging task. Aside from the fact that there are intense debates (though not public ones) in the PRC about the goals the country should be trying to attain and the best way of achieving them, today's thinkers draw on a range of historical resources, not just ancient but including more recent historical experiences of revolution and reform and the ever-present Western concepts which underpin much of the present-day international system.

Precisely how China's rather eclectic approach to foreign and security policy will play out therefore remains to be seen, including in relation to Taiwan (which MacDonald discusses in detail). Sun Tzu may not have all the answers, as noted below (p. 122). But given its prominence in the world views and studies of China's strategists, this treatise should be read and understood by anyone wishing to gain insights into the 21st-century objectives of the PRC. This new translation and commentary offers an excellent resource to help us in this endeavour.

Dr. Tim Summers
The Chinese University of Hong Kong and Chatham House

PREFACE

THE CHINESE CLASSIC commonly known in English as *The Art of War* has multiple identities. As one of the earliest-known texts circulated among a widely dispersed readership anywhere, it is an object of historical and bibliographical scrutiny. It is on the curricula of the world's leading military academies, and is cited for the perspective it brings to contemporary geostrategic issues. It is studied by scholars and truth-seekers as a philosophical treatise. And it is the inspiration for a wealth of titles in the publishing industry's learning-and-development category, in the guise of Sun Tzu-themed spin-offs for business, sport, relationships and more. Yet despite the work's diverse appeal, it is widely misunderstood. This book, and the new translation it contains, aims to correct that.

The original work, dating from the decades before and after 300 BC, was the most systematic exploration of military philosophy, strategy and tactics of its era, and to this day it remains probably the most profound and comprehensive single volume on these topics. It was written in and for a world of sophisticated, heavily-populated states, by turns co-operating and competing with each other while locked in an interminable arms race—a world arguably not so different from ours. This helps to explain why the treatise still offers startling insights into the struggles and strategies of nations.

The language of Sun Tzu is dense and economical, in the manner characteristic of early Classical Chinese. The text was intended not solely to be read, but also to be recited, construed, taught and discussed. Ellipsis and allusion were part of its rhetorical fabric, but the goal was to clarify, not to baffle. This is well appreciated in the Chinese-speaking world, where the treatise has generally been regarded as coherent and comprehensible. Not so in the West, however, where commentators and translators have tended to lament the text's thematic discontinuities and seemingly patchwork assembly. The solution, in translation, has conventionally been to re-imagine the work as a repository of wise aphorisms on an ancient "art", rather than as the lucid compilation of practical military guidance that it is.

What Sun Tzu mapped out, for his 3rd-century BC audience, was a conceptual framework for the study and practice of the fast-developing discipline of mass-population interstate warfare. He packaged and presented a systematic body of empirically derived knowledge which, in today's terms, would be considered more of a "science" than an "art". This is the first translation in English to recognize that distinction, and will, it is hoped, make this celebrated classic more readable and intelligible in English than ever before.

The translation is preceded by essays on the Warring States period (5th century BC to 221 BC) in which the treatise emerged, along with analysis of a number of military campaigns from the past two millennia in which at least one side was probably aware of and influenced by Sun Tzu. These include campaigns waged by Cao Cao at the turn of the 3rd century, Genghis Khan in the 13th century and Napoleon in the early 19th century. We also trace Sun Tzu's strategic lineage through to the military and political convulsions of the 20th century.

Part One of the book concludes with an in-depth examination of Sun Tzu's influence on the People's Republic of China (PRC), and in particular on the geostrategic priorities of the Chinese

Communist Party (CCP).

For military theorists of the Warring States period, Sun Tzu foremost among them, friction among nations was always a potential prelude to war, and had to be managed in the same planned, pragmatic, devious way that an army tries to govern the situation in the run-up to battle. That Warring States paradigm of interstate conflict is woven into nationalist narratives that the CCP now relies on to assert its right to rule China, and elements of Sun Tzu can be seen in the PRC's grand strategic hostility towards the United States and Japan, its creeping campaign to monopolize the South China Sea, and its increasingly credible threats against Taiwan. For China's neighbours in East Asia, and for military and strategic planners in the US, it is now more important than ever to know and understand Sun Tzu.

The teachings of Sun Tzu can be applied in many ways and in many domains. The treatise undoubtedly provides military thinkers with a practical compendium of strategy and tactics. But to what degree it offers a suitable guide for action on the world stage today, whether by the PRC or any other nation, remains an open question.

Christopher MacDonald
Cardiff
November 2017

PART ONE

1
Sun Tzu the man
and *Sun-tzu* the text

FROM THE OPENING line of Sun Tzu's Science of War we are invited
to imagine that we are holding a posthumously transcribed
compilation of oral teachings delivered long ago by an esteemed
strategist. This was as true for readers in ancient China as it is
today. Each chapter opens with the phrase "Sun Tzu states...", and
early readers of the text were taught to identify Sun Tzu ("Master
Sun" in English) as one Sun Wu, a military adviser to the erstwhile
kingdom of Wu during the period when that kingdom had been at
the peak of its power.

Historians in later eras, having scoured the records for
evidence of Sun Wu, came to doubt his existence, and speculation
arose that the text may have instead originated among the
writings of one Sun Bin, a general and military theorist who was
active in the 4th century BC, around one-and-a-half centuries
after the kingdom of Wu's demise.

More recently, textual analysis has pointed to the possibility
that neither Sun Wu nor Sun Bin could have been behind the
treatise, and that it must have originated as a compendium of
military lore, transcribed over a span of decades by unknown
hands. Whatever the truth, the traditional tale about the work's
origins in the teachings of Sun Wu offers valuable insights into
the way that a science of war began to take shape in ancient China

during a period of remarkable military transition.

Sun Wu – the first Master Sun

In the centuries before the first fully centralized empire was forged in the eastern part of what is now China, the region was a patchwork of principalities and city states, each nominally sworn in fealty to the royal house of Zhou. In the mid-eighth century BC, there were around 170 such polities, clustered north and south of the Yellow River in an area half the size of Western Europe today. They battled and merged as Zhou authority dissolved, and by the late sixth century BC around a dozen large states remained, plus a handful of satellites. One of those states was the kingdom of Wu,[1] which is where the Sun Tzu story traditionally begins.

Wu was located hundreds of miles south-east of the Zhou heartland, and encompassed the alluvial plain where the Yangtze River feeds into the sea — the region that now includes the cities of Shanghai and Suzhou. It was a land of rivers and wetlands, in a part of the world that, until a few generations earlier, had been considered barbarian. Barbarian in that its regional chieftains lacked lineage links to the royal house of Zhou, its ruling clans did not rely on the common script and canon of rites that knit the Zhou nobility together, and its people were short on the technology, towns, correct feudal hierarchy and proper customs that marked the civilized realm of what were known as the "central states".[2]

By the late sixth century BC, however, the people and rulers of Wu had largely assimilated to "civilization". From the Zhou perspective they remained backwards, yet backwardness can have consolations for an up-and-coming nation under energetic

---

1   Written as *wú* (吳) in Chinese pinyin, and unrelated to the *wǔ* (武) in the name "Sun Wu".
2   The "central states", or *zhōngguó* (中國), as the core Zhou states considered themselves, gives modern China its name for itself.

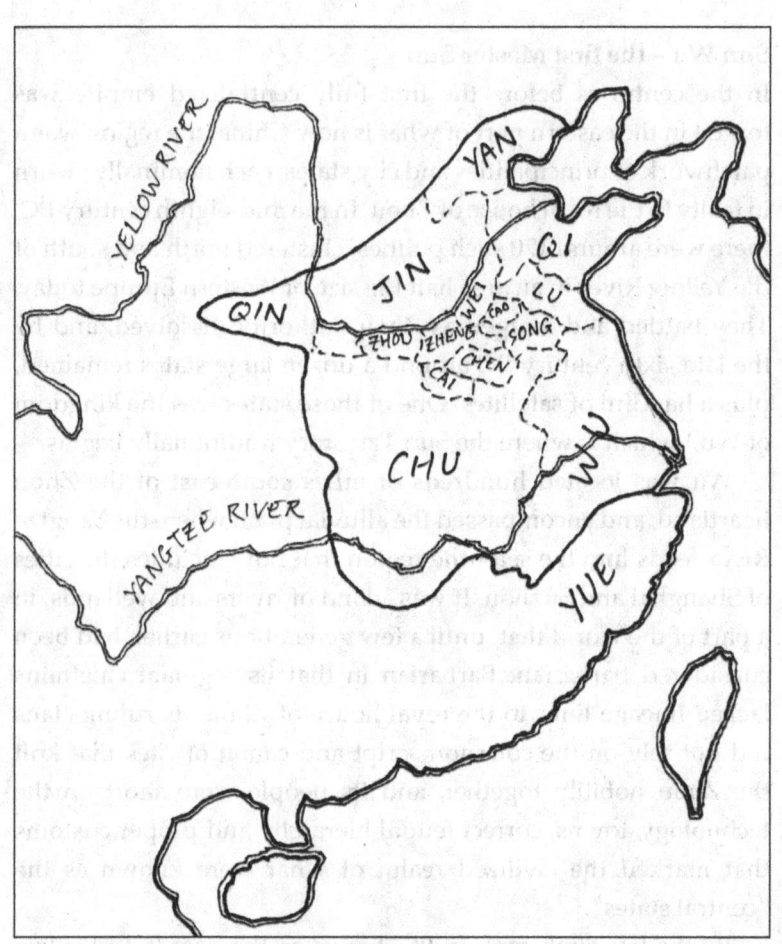

Map 1

The Zhou realm in the 6th century BC

Sun Wu reputedly hailed from a military clan in the state of Qi (in the area of present-day Shandong province) and moved to the state of Wu (centred on the lower reaches of the Yangtze River), for advancement, in the late 6th century BC. The state of Wu was wealthy and ambitious, but was regarded as an uncouth outsider by the "central states" clustered along the Yellow River to the north. However, Wu's conquest of Chu, under Sun Wu's strategic guidance, in 506 BC, elevated the state to a position of dominance, and its king became the recognized "hegemon" of the Zhou realm. Wu held that position until 473 BC when it was overrun and erased from the map by its southern neighbour, Yue.

leaders who opt for wholesale importation of successful ideas, technology and organizational methods from their more developed neighbours. Wu already enjoyed significant economic assets in the form of fertile terrain and warm climate suitable for highly productive wet-rice farming, along with abundant deposits of the ores used to make bronze, a metal prized among the Zhou elites for ceremonial wares and weapons. The kingdom had quickly became a prosperous and dynamic addition to the Zhou realm.

One of Wu's most significant imports at this time was military expertise, with talented army professionals attracted to the upstart kingdom by opportunities for wealth and advancement. Towards the end of the sixth century BC, Wu's ambitious, expansion-minded sovereign, King Helü (reigned 514–496 BC), having seized power by assassinating his predecessor, set his sights on the state of Chu, Wu's overbearing neighbour to the west, in the region now covered by Hubei province.

Chu was a super-state, the largest in territory and population that there had ever been in the world of ancient China. Like Wu, it had taken shape along the barbarous southern periphery of the Zhou heartland and was a relative latecomer to civilization. Being closer to the heartland than Wu, Chu had assimilated earlier and then battled its way to supremacy, eventually earning its king paramount status among the Zhou sovereigns. Chu was top dog, but by the late sixth century BC it was experiencing the drawbacks of size and supremacy such as decadence at court, internecine conflict among powerful clans, calcified institutions of governance and a general decline in the appetite for opportunity and risk that characterizes states on the rise.

Under Helü's aggressive leadership, the kingdom of Wu began chipping away at the Chu borderlands. In 506 BC, a string of victories for the Wu armies culminated with the sacking of the

Chu capital of Ying, located near what is now the city of Jingzhou in central Hubei. It is with this campaign that history, whether credibly or not, first records the involvement of a commander and strategist called Sun Wu, or "Sun-the-Martial".

Sun Wu (c. 544–496 BC) arrived in the kingdom of Wu as an émigré from one of the core Zhou states to the north. He came from an established army family and had a good reputation as a soldier and strategist. His potted biography, recorded around four centuries later in what became ancient China's definitive work of history, Sima Qian's *Historical Records*, written around the year 100 BC, tells of how he was introduced to King Helü by a senior minister, and then, by an astonishing feat of audacity, secured a senior military command for himself.

The story goes that Helü challenged Sun, already celebrated for his thirteen-part treatise on warfare, to drill the palace ladies in basic marching skills, while king and court observed from a pavilion terrace. Sun separated the ladies — 180 of them — into two companies, each headed by one of the king's favourite concubines. He showed them how to hold a halberd (a pole-mounted blade) and issued formal instructions on turning to the left, the right, the front and the back in response to signals from the drum. He had a broad-ax placed at the front as a marker of discipline. His first attempt to signal the moves ended with the ladies giggling. He repeated his instructions the approved number of times, and started over. Again, giggles. The regulation penalty for failure to carry out clearly expressed orders, Sun solemnly announced, was to be the beheading of the company commanders.

At this point, Helü hastily sent a messenger down to the parade ground to tell Sun that the king was particularly fond of the two ladies concerned, and to note that since Sun had already made his point, there was no need to proceed with

9

the executions. Sun sent back a message stating that as chief commander, appointed on sovereign authority, he was obliged to disregard certain interventions in military matters from even the monarch. He had the king's favourites beheaded, appointed the next two in line as company commanders, and resumed the drill.

This time the ladies marched to perfection, with not a whisper to be heard. Sun sent another message to the king confirming that the "troops" were ready for him to inspect, and that they would obey any order he cared to give. The king despondently declined the inspection, and Sun was told to return to his quarters. Helü subsequently appointed Sun to a position of senior military command and the kingdom went on to claim a string of military successes.

This startling tale reveals something about the way Sun Tzu was associated in that era with the emergence of a new mode of military organization during a period of intensifying military and social transition. The notional Master Sun presents the king with an apparently unfamiliar paradigm of military command in which discipline is supreme, in which even the most hopeless soldierly material can be drilled to perfection, and in which the senior commander's writ is law. Moreover, the senior commander in this new military paradigm is not the valorous, weapon-wielding warrior-prince of Zhou tradition, who charges gloriously into battle at the head of his chariot-mounted nobles, but rather a baton-waving drillmaster who orchestrates, from his vantage point, the trained maneuvers of conscript infantry. This new breed of commander is privy to a powerful source of secret knowledge in the form of a written text, which codifies the bewildering complexity of war in the language of rules and principles, knowledge which an ambitious, hawkish sovereign could not afford to ignore.

By not promptly executing Sun for his defiance, King Helü

symbolically accepts the new system of military values, thereby gaining access to Sun Wu's professional knowledge. He is rewarded by conquering Chu and achieving dominion over the entire Zhou realm.

In reality, the paradigm shift reflected in this story took place over several centuries, as warfare transitioned from the Zhou convention of limited-scale confrontation fought to a chivalric code between the nobility of small, agrarian polities, to an early version of what we would now consider "total war" — war fought on multiple fronts with massive infantry armies fielded by heavily militarized states capable of mobilizing entire populations.

Traditionally among the Zhou states, warfare had been the preserve of the male aristocracy, a ritually sanctioned spilling of blood by which the main combatants displayed valour and virility, and thereby affirmed their right to rule. Battles were restricted to windows in the agricultural and astrological calendars, and were contained in scale because it was impractical for small states with limited hinterland and rudimentary institutions to train and mobilize big armies. Commoners, usually untrained, were present on the battlefield only in an auxiliary capacity. They carried basic weapons of wood or stone, often farm implements, wore little or no armour, and jogged into battle alongside the chariot-borne nobles who were expensively equipped, often with bronze weapons and lacquered, leather body armour.

A typical "war" involved a one-off battle, its date and location agreed in advance, with at most a few thousand men on either side. After the battle, survivors would return to their respective settlements and life would go on much as before, even if the outcome of the conflict had involved a transfer of territorial title among ruling clans.

For the aristocratic protagonists, the primary aim of battle was to win martial glory, and to earn honour and prestige in the eyes of their peers and posterity. Failure to fight in the approved manner would undermine that goal, so it was not unknown for combatants to spare the lives of their opponents and pass up an opportunity for victory rather than transgress chivalric code.

But by the sixth century BC, that model of conflict was becoming redundant, and the purpose of war was in the late stages of transitioning from "glory at all costs," through "victory with glory," to "victory at all costs." Wealthy super-states were by now competing for control over extensive territories and populations of millions, and the scale of armed conflict among them was rapidly escalating.

The peripheral, fast-rising kingdom of Wu, less constrained by Zhou tradition, seized the opportunity of this transition to translate its fast-growing political and economic clout into military strength and territorial gains. Wu's conflict with its massive neighbour Chu, the dominant power of the age, turned out therefore to be the testing ground for a dramatic new direction in armed conflict. This was not yet the archetypal Sun Tzu variety of warfare, which took another century or so to develop, but in strategy and tactics, as well as in organizational efficiency, the Wu armies displayed recognizable elements of an approach to armed conflict that was to become universal.

During the six years from 512 to 506 BC, Wu seized several of Chu's client states, making ample use of tactical subterfuge and surprise attacks, then retreating when necessary to avoid being drawn into any decisive engagement with superior Chu forces. One effect of Wu's sustained campaign of provocation was to exacerbate divisions among Chu's ruling and military factions, which disagreed as to how to interpret and respond to Wu's actions. All the while, the Wu armies were gearing up for a planned full-scale onslaught, drilling rigorously in the disciplines of segmenting, merging, signals and maneuvers.

Having undermined Chu's military confidence in this way for six years, Wu baited its foe with a three-pronged advance from the north, meanwhile massing for a larger invasion from the south, where Wu could profit from logistical support and military intelligence supplied by new allies in the border regions. Chu's main defensive force initially marched north, then hastily revised its objective and raced south, only to be defeated and driven back by the invaders' disciplined, tightly-coordinated, well-motivated army. A decisive defeat at the Battle of Boju in present-day Hubei province turned the Chu retreat into a rout, and Wu drove forward to seize the Chu capital. The Boju campaign, as it came to be recorded, was, for its era, an unprecedented feat of logistics and organization as well as a triumph of strategy and tactics, and was celebrated as the first successful, sustained, long-distance campaign of its type in Chinese history.

Boju was the culmination of a planned process marked by some of the strategic and tactical approaches for which Sun Tzu was later renowned. These included the long-game grand strategy by which Wu softened up Chu for invasion while stealthily gathering intelligence and building alliances; the focus on training, discipline, coordination and mobility, which gave Wu forces the flexibility to divide and out-maneuver the larger, lumbering Chu armies; the practised habit of seizing the initiative and attacking fast, while retaining the option to retreat in good order when circumstances were not in Wu's favour; and that calculated gamble on the bold ruse, wrong-footing Chu with a dummy invasion from one end of country while attacking with a larger force at the other end. As the Wu leadership correctly surmised, Chu was more vulnerable than it appeared, and quickly succumbed to the invader's combination of single-minded strategy plus determined attack.

Boju turned out to be a tipping point in Zhou China's centuries-long slide into the rampant militarism of the Warring States period (fifth century BC to 221 BC), the start of an era of relentless campaigns fought between giant, complex states mobilizing whole populations and fielding mass-infantry armies of up to half a million men.

By the time of Boju, chivalry was vanishing into history as strategic and tactical subterfuge became the norm. At the same time, the pressure towards larger, more disciplined armies was giving rise to a new class of military professionals — the commanders, planners and administrators whose lineage placed them outside the traditional, hereditary hierarchy of military command and control, but whose specialist skills were vital to army operations and who were therefore able to market their talents wherever they were in demand.

Sun Wu, whether fictional or not, stands as an early example of the type. More technocrat than aristocrat, Sun Wu was a military specialist head-hunted for his expertise in shaping reluctant peasantry into disciplined infantry units. King Helü and his senior ministers would certainly have needed advice on military organization and tactics during the years of preparation to invade Chu, and it is easy to picture one of those experts as being, like Sun Wu, the scion of an established military clan from one of the status quo powers of the Zhou heartland along the Yellow River.

With their dry climate and cultivated plains, the Yellow River states had long since evolved a regimented model of warfare suited to chariot charges and, latterly, to infantry campaigns. In the Yangtze River regions of the south, by contrast, with their more recent "barbarian" heritage and terrain of marshes, lakes, mountains and forests, war remained closer to its origins in the form of local brigandage and feuding. Bandit cunning, surprise, speed, tactical flexibility, the ability to rapidly exploit opportunities, and the willingness to turn tail and flee when clearly outnumbered or outwitted, were still in the region's fighting DNA, relatively unhindered by the aristocratic proprieties of the Zhou. On the other hand, the rulers in this southern region were relatively short on the expertise needed to scale up military forces by mass conscription, and to effectively manage the far larger armies that were required for the new era of warfare.

The Sun Wu of fable is therefore a plausible hybrid. An elite northerner in the service of an uncouth southern state; an innovator who fused northern method and structure with southern flair and flexibility to create a new system of warfare; and the founder of the embryonic science of armed conflict, detailed in his treatise, the secrets of which propelled the kingdom of Wu to the zenith of power.

Apocryphal or otherwise, the story of Sun Wu and his association with the system of thinking that underpins the *Suntzu*, offers an important insight into the transition to the Warring States period, as the Zhou states battled and converged into a single, highly militarized empire.

Sun Bin – the second Master Sun
The story of Sun Wu – the first Sun Tzu – places him at an early juncture in the transition from the age of chivalry to that of total war, but the story of Sun Bin – the second Sun Tzu – comes close to the end of that transition, when the stately conventions of feudal warfare had almost completely given way to the militarist approach depicted in the famous treatise.

Sun Bin (c. 380–316 BC) is a reasonably well-attested historical figure whose biography immediately follows that of Sun Wu in Sima Qian's *Historical Records*. He was, according

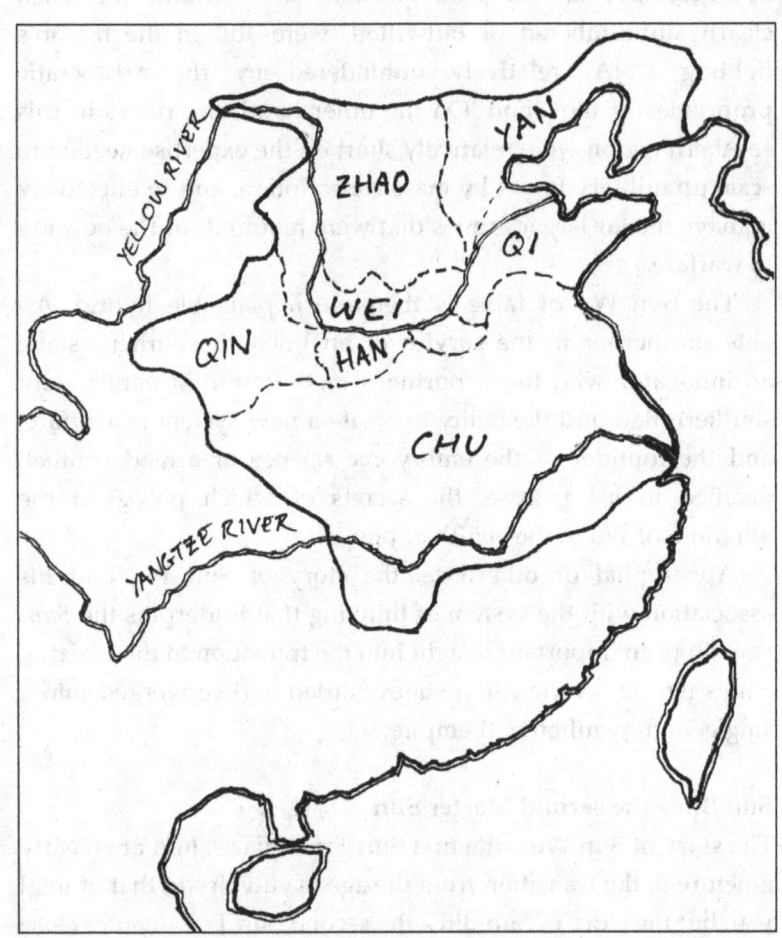

Map 2

The Warring States circa 350 BC

States battled and merged, and by around 350 BC there were seven major states still standing. Sun Bin, reputedly Sun Wu's descendant, was one of the most renowned strategists of the age. The defining struggle of his career, against his comrade-turned-rival Pang Juan, culminated in 342 BC, when Sun Bin led the Qi army to victory over the army of Wei under Pang.

By this time, the Westernmost of the seven states, Qin, had already begun implementing the "legalist" economic and political reforms that were to set it on a course of unstoppable military expansion, culminating with its conquest of the entire Zhou realm in 221 BC. Legalism, moderated by a Confucian moral code, remains the guiding mode of state governance in China to this day.

to Sima Qian, a direct descendant of the earlier Sun, and made his name in the service of the same powerful northern state, the kingdom of Qi, from which Sun Wu originally hailed. He was the outstanding strategist of the mid-Warring States period, around 150 years after Sun Wu, and his campaigns combined bandit guile with organizational sophistication, a hallmark of the Sun Tzu approach. He also wrote prolifically on military theory, though most of the works posthumously attributed to him, some circulated in the name Sun Bin and some in the name Sun Tzu, have been lost to posterity.

Sun Bin's most celebrated victory, at Maling (in present-day Henan province) in 342 BC, was a showdown with his estranged comrade, Pang Juan, who commanded the army of the kingdom of Wei. Years earlier, Pang had framed Sun for some (unrecorded) crime, in punishment for which Sun's legs were mutilated and his face tattooed — Sun Bin means "Sun-the-kneecapped". Sun subsequently directed military operations from a covered wagon away from the action.

The troops of Qi had a reputation, among the Wei, for being pusillanimous while on campaign beyond their borders. Sun played on this perception as he slowly withdrew from Wei territory by arranging for his troops to light 100,000 cooking fires on their first night, 50,000 fires on the second night and 30,000 on the third night. Pang Juan, flushed with confidence following a recent victory over an ally of the kingdom of Qi's and emboldened by his scouts' reports that Qi troops were deserting in droves, decided to accelerate his plans for engaging the enemy.

Leaving behind the main body of his infantry, Pang mustered a lightly-armed contingent of elite troops and raced two days' distance in a single day, confident of crushing the Qi army. Sun meanwhile rested his troops, estimated the speed of Pang's advance, and concealed 10,000 crossbowmen in a wooded pass among the hills. At the anticipated hour, just past nightfall, the Wei troops marched into the ambush and a hail of crossbow fire. Pang was killed or committed suicide and his troops were thrown into confusion. The Qi army followed up by destroying the main body of Pang's army and went on to subjugate Wei.

Sun Bin's victory at Maling displayed a characteristic Sun Tzu blend of strategic planning combined with a skilfully executed tactical ruse. Above all, Sun understood and successfully manipulated his opponent's psychology. He guessed successfully that the Wei high command would jump to conclusions when the scouts observed the diminishing number of cooking fires, and his familiarity with Pang enabled him to predict an over-confident response. Sure enough, Pang's military zeal and visceral loathing of Sun clouded his judgement at the critical hour. In his haste to pounce, Pang raced into an ambush and an unnecessary battle for which he was ill-equipped. Having eliminated the Wei commanding general and tipped the strategic balance decisively in his favour, Sun was then able to finish off the remainder of the Wei army and seize control of the country.

At the time when Sun Bin defeated Pang Juan and the Wei army, there were seven competing states left standing, each with war as its central organizing principle. It was, by then, normal for states to field conscript armies of 100,000 or more men, supported for months at a time by complex logistical arrangements, with command exercised through a hierarchy of professional officers headed by an autonomous field marshal and supported by a full-time military bureaucracy. Military organization on this scale tallies exactly with the world depicted in the *Sun-tzu*, but would have been exceptional or impossible around 150 years earlier, in Sun Wu's day, when the largest armies are thought to have numbered only 40,000 men.

Furthermore, the standard weaponry and military technology

mentioned in the treatise, including crossbows and siege machines, match those of Sun Bin's era but not Sun Wu's, and this argues for the text being produced later rather than earlier. The treatise also includes references to still earlier military writings which could not have existed during the time of Sun Wu (there is no evidence of military theory, or any comparable professional knowledge, being recorded and circulated in written form during the time of Sun Wu) but which could conceivably have been in circulation by the time that Sun Bin was active.

It is worth noting that Sun Bin was often referred to, in later writings, as Sun Tzu, or "Master Sun", and was closely associated with the strategic and tactical approaches described in the *Sun-tzu*, in particular its core concept of military potency or "strategic dominance" (*shi*, 勢). Sun Bin could, therefore, have been the real Sun Tzu behind the famous treatise, and if he wasn't, the text does at least appear to have been a product of his era, in the middle of the Warring States period, and not of that time one-and-a-half centuries earlier, when Sun Wu met King Helü and helped the kingdom of Wu to conquer Chu. Not only did the concrete and strategic realities of Sun Bin's day match those of the Sun Tzu treatise, but Sun Bin's world was also one in which there was a market for words of wisdom from renowned military figures, packaged and distributed in the new medium of the scrolled book.

The text emerges — a tale of two Master Suns
Linguistic and stylistic analysis of Warring States texts supports the theory that the *Sun-tzu* was composed largely during the second half of the fourth century BC, and moreover indicates that its chapters originated as individual tracts. Those tracts were drafted over a span of decades in the thick of the Warring States transition, a period of intensifying armed conflict that would

end, around a century later, with consolidation into the empire that became China. The datings suggest that the first chapter-tracts emerged while Sun Bin was in his professional prime, as a practitioner and a theorist.

The Sun Bin hypothesis is countered, however, by two references in the *Sun-tzu* to the bitter rivalry between the kingdoms of Wu and Yue (ch. 6.5 and ch. 11.4, in this translation), a conflict which ended with Wu's annexation by Yue in 473 BC. Sun Wu could conceivably have used that rivalry as a contemporary point of reference in his teachings, but Sun Bin, writing nearly one-and-half centuries after Wu was permanently erased from the map, could not. Another anomaly is that the *Sun-tzu* includes several prominent references to chariot warfare, something that was common among the Zhou states of Sun Wu's time, but was on the way out in favour of mass-infantry armies in Sun Bin's day. There is also the fact that Sun Bin's detailed attention to the techniques of siege warfare, in various fragments of text attributed to him, contradict the disdain for sieges that is expressed by Sun Tzu (ch. 3.2).

In support of the doubts about Sun Bin's involvement with the "Master Sun" treatise, we might also ask why only some of his writings assumed that honorific title, while others continued to be circulated separately in the name Sun Bin, as if Master Sun and Sun Bin were two different people. And how did the Master Sun portion of Sun Bin's corpus, having been uncoupled from the memory of the celebrated general, get attached instead to the story of a lesser-known and possibly apocryphal figure, in the person of Sun Wu?

All we can say for sure is that there was a scrambling of identity between Sun Wu, Sun Bin, and "Master Sun" during the hundred years or so between the second half of the fourth century BC, when the first tracts were composed, and the second half of the third century BC as the Warring States period came to an end. This may even have been a deliberate feature of the writings from the moment they entered circulation.

Unfortunately, we cannot be sure how that scrambling of identities occurred because most of the documentary record for the period went up in flames. In 213 BC, the first Qin emperor approved a decree ordering the empire-wide burning of various categories of privately-held texts, including technical and philosophical treatises on warfare. The disastrous effect of this decree for historical scholarship was compounded seven years later, as the regime crumbled, when rebels razed the imperial archives, destroying yet more texts and records.

The only reliable trace of Sun Tzu materials from the pre-Qin period is found in the *Lüshi Chunqiu* (呂氏春秋), an encyclopaedic work from around 240 BC, which survived the book burnings intact. One section refers in passing to the military methods advocated by "Sun and Wu" (the Wu in this pairing alludes to Wu Qi, a statesman-general who reputedly authored a military classic known as the *Wuzi*), and associates the pair with King Helü, while another section names Sun Bin among a series of influential thinkers from earlier times, and states that he "emphasized [the concept of] strategic dominance [in his teachings]".

For the authors and readers of the *Lüshi Chunqiu* encyclopaedia, "Sun and Wu" evidently formed a byword for military expertise, which strongly suggests that the writings of one or other of the Suns were by that time widely known and held in high regard. This impression is compounded by references to Sun in other texts ostensibly from the pre-Qin period (before 221 BC), though less reliably dated given that they were extensively revised, or even recreated from memory and fragments of text, in the years following the Qin convulsion. As one of those writings, a compendium of Legalist philosophy called the *Hanfeizi*, reports: "Everyone in the country discusses military matters, and every family keeps copies of the books of Sun and Wu."

What we can say with confidence is that by start of the second century BC at the latest, the Master Sun tracts had coalesced (or been purposefully integrated) into a single, widely-circulated edition. Moreover we can infer from archaeological findings that by the middle of that century, the 13-chapter Master Sun treatise was unequivocally attributed to Sun Wu, the fabled strategist whose guidance had helped King Helü conquer the Kingdom of Chu, nearly four centuries earlier, and not to his notional descendant Sun Bin.

The earliest surviving copy of the *Sun-tzu* was excavated in 1972 from a Han dynasty tomb, in Linyi county, Shandong province, in what was once the Warring States kingdom of Qi – the ancestral homeland of both Sun Wu and Sun Bin. The tomb dates from the period 140-118 BC but the manuscript itself is older, possibly by several decades.

A book, at that time, comprised bamboo slats (each a little wider and longer than a chopstick) bound into rolls by silk thread, with script written top-to-bottom in soot-black ink. The threads of the Linyi manuscript have rotted away and a few of the slats are missing, but it is likely that there would have been around two-hundred slats, bundled into three rolls, for the complete text of the *Sun-tzu*.

Also retrieved at the same site were supplementary Master Sun materials, from which it is apparent that readers of the time were aware of a distinction between two historical military figures with the family name Sun, both of whom had produced authoritative works on strategy, and both of whom had merited the title "Sun Tzu".

Between two and four decades after the Linyi tombs were

sealed, the Han dynasty Grand Historian Sima Qian (c. 145-86 BC) completed the *Historical Records*, in which the biography of the earlier Sun Tzu – identified for the first time on record as Sun Wu – was succeeded directly by the biography of Sun Bin, whom Sima Qian describes as Sun Wu's descendant. Both the Sun Tzu treatise and Sun Bin's own eponymous treatise, continued to be extant for most of the Han dynasty, judging by the catalogues of the imperial archives, but by the time the Han dynasty disintegrated into civil war around AD 200 , the Sun Bin treatise appears to have been lost, and it remained lost right up until the discoveries at Linyi in 1972.

Meanwhile, the *Sun-tzu* was taken up and championed by Cao Cao (AD 155–220), the warlord-statesman who dominated the era of the Han collapse, and his annotated commentary canonized the treatise for future generations, cementing the tradition that it had originated with the teachings of Sun Wu. Cao's version of the treatise, complete with annotations, formed the basis for woodblock-print editions commissioned during the Song dynasty (960-1279), one of which became the received version transmitted down to the modern age, with minor amendments following the discoveries at Linyi.

So, was the first Sun, "Sun-the-Martial", the presiding spirit of the *Sun-tzu*, or was it the second Sun, "Sun-the-Kneecapped"? Or both, or neither? And how much difference does it make for our understanding of the text?

If it was Sun Wu, the first Master Sun, then we may imagine his teachings being orally transmitted down the generations, within his clan or among his followers, until that point in the middle of the Warring States period when person or persons unknown began to transcribe those teachings for a wider audience. Those persons, while channelling the spirit of the old commander, may well have updated the content for the readers of their day, introducing contemporary weaponry and military organizational features, yet retaining historical features such as those references to the long-gone rivalry between the kingdoms of Wu and Yue.

But if it was Sun Bin, the second Master Sun, then we may imagine the teachings of the celebrated general and military theorist being transcribed and circulated over a span of decades during the Warring States period, and then, whether by accident or design, becoming separated from the memory of Sun Bin and associated instead with his possibly apocryphal forebear. The age was turbulent enough to account for that separation to have taken place by accident, and if it was by design, then we need only envisage a scenario in which Sun Bin or later editors and archivists opted for a veneer of classical pedigree, by presenting the content as the teachings of a long-dead military guru, and deliberately inserting the Wu-Yue conflict and chariot warfare references for verisimilitude. There was, after all, no precedent in Sun Bin's day for men of influence to draft and circulate writings in their own name, and it may well have invited trouble to do so.

Could the text even have been the product of both men's teachings?

Yes, if one conceives of Sun Bin editing and updating the work of his storied ancestor, at the same time as accumulating a separate corpus under his own name.

Or alternatively, could it have been the work of neither man, but rather the brainchild of a determined compiler of existing military lore, who created or borrowed the Master Sun persona for credibility and attention? Again, yes, although he would have been an outstanding military personage in his own right, judging by the depth and authoritativeness of the work, and might just as well have been one or other of the original Master Sun candidates.

Each scenario is plausible in its way, but in a sense the matter is academic. The historical significance of the *Sun-tzu* lies less in the question of authorship, and more in the mixed identity it has had since being released by its final editors, addressing us as it does from two separate points in time.

The treatise speaks partly from the time of Sun Wu, as its compiler-editors evidently wished readers of the day to believe. That had been a pivotal point in the history of war, when a semi-barbarian king, craving honour among the established states yet unafraid to cheat the rules of engagement, successfully merged his region's traditions of martial cunning and mobility with the military discipline and organizational structure needed for the new era of mass-infantry warfare.

And it speaks partly from the time of Sun Bin, in the middle of the Warring States period, when the teachings in the treatise first crystallized into written form. The chivalric mode of warfare had by then yielded to a new approach founded on rationally structured systems of organization, in which winning was everything and individual glory was of little consequence. Infantry armies had multiplied in scale and complexity, and the carnage when they clashed had grown correspondingly. The management of war had become an industry, a huge and complex business requiring a class of specialists, who very much needed textual resources of the kind offered by treatises such as Sun Tzu's.

Sun Wu, whether legendary or otherwise, was an early incarnation of the military professional. He was a seasoned commander and organizational expert, but also a man of discipline and courage, willing to chance an excruciating death in a bid to advance his career.

His notional descendant Sun Bin, by contrast, was the exemplar of the modern commanding officer—a literate strategist and skilled army manager, who planned and guided his campaigns from his command post set back from the front line.

The *Sun-tzu* treatise, which channels the wisdom and experience of both men, therefore has much to tell us about how the science of war was understood and applied at its formative stage during China's Warring States transition.

2
Art of War or science of war?

There may well be an art to war, just as there is an art to government and an art to life, a body of skills and principles typically acquired through experience and taught by example. But art is not the focus of the *Sun-tzu*.

The work's title in standard romanized Chinese is *Sunzi Bingfa* (孫子兵法), and that term *bingfa* (兵法) combines a Chinese character indicating weaponry, soldiers and armed conflict, with one connoting method, or a system of rules and principles. In classical times the pairing formed a generic term for any functional treatise on applied military matters. *Bingfa* texts explained campaign and battlefield tactics alongside the logistical, institutional and political dimensions of war. In structure and content they were designed to provide practical guidance, in the form of strategic principles governing the overall approach to war combined with specific techniques to use before and during the fight. The thinkers whose views came to be disseminated in the *bingfa* form, offered commanders a tool for prioritizing their energies and resources during the run-up to war, along with a menu of practical methods for winning war.

The Sun Tzu treatise was not the first of its kind, though it is the earliest to have survived the wholesale destruction of manuscripts that occurred in the Qin dynasty (221–206 BC). It was also the most succinct, comprehensive and best structured *bingfa* of the era, offering systematic analysis of operational tactics combined with the first-known outline theory of military strategy. In effect, Sun Tzu pioneered the science of war.

Structure
As discussed in the preceding section of Part One, analysis of

the text indicates that each of the thirteen chapters in the *Sun-tzu* originated as a standalone tract before being integrated into the work we know today. Each chapter focuses on a particular aspect of warfare, and does so from the perspective of a commander at the head of a massive Warring States (5th century to 221 BC) army, tasked with the challenge of extracting victory from among the chaotic currents of interstate conflict. In sequence, the thirteen chapters broadly track the process of preparing for and then engaging in armed conflict, providing commanders with a programme for rational military management while also offering philosophical insight into the irrational and in many ways unmanageable nature of war.

The first seven chapters of the treatise place the events of war in their strategic context—the battle as part of a campaign, and the campaign as part of a wider pattern of confrontation. Preparation begins with early empirical analysis of the overall situation and proceeds to the shaping of a strategic landscape that favours victory for your side. The next four chapters cover a compendium of operational and tactical considerations, mostly related to maneuvers, terrain and environmental factors, while the final two chapters are specialist tutorials on incendiary attacks and intelligence operations.

Within this framework, there is a degree of overspill between chapters and plenty of digression. For example, Chapter 10 of the treatise, entitled "Terrain", begins with a classification of terrain types before digressing to list a series of circumstances, attributable to poor leadership, in which armies capitulate. After briefly returning to the topic of terrain, the chapter veers off again to discuss key character traits of a chief commander, then concludes with a short disquisition on the relationship between knowledge and victory.

Every chapter in the *Sun-tzu* contains off-topic statements and sections, often patched into place with the aid of conjunctive characters meaning "so...", "hence..." or "in this way...". For the purpose of this translation, sub-headings and spacing are inserted between passages to signal switches of theme and topic. Nevertheless, the liveliness which the narrative skips around can be confusing.

The sometimes indiscriminate succession of ideas in part reflects the manner, more than 2,000 years ago, in which writings were stitched together and amended, often over the course of generations. At a number of points in the text, characters from an unknown earlier edition have clearly gone astray or been wrongly transcribed, and several passages of the treatise appear to have been wrongly interpolated or loosely copied from earlier chapters.

But thematic free-association was also one of the rhetorical conventions of classical Chinese, which allowed writers to express their thinking in a non-linear fashion. Key assertions were to be circled over and presented from various angles so that readers could probe for connections and anomalies while bringing their own perspectives to bear. Moreover, a "reader" in classical times was just as likely to be a listener, with the text presented orally and construed character by character and phrase by phrase, in the presence of a tutor or in discussion with other readers.

For modern readers, in a Western language, this is an unfamiliar approach to constructing a written argument and it can be an obstacle to understanding. In China, by contrast, the *Sun-tzu* has generally been regarded as structurally and conceptually coherent, and well worth its reputation as the ancient world's most profound and intelligible text on the principles of warfare.

That coherence resides partly in the text's presentational tone — the tone of the commander and strategist known as Master Sun — and partly in the structural and conceptual fabric of the work. Structural, in terms of the sequence of chapters, and the ordered presentation of information within individual passages, typically involving classified lists. Conceptual, in terms of a handful of core ideas which are woven throughout the text.

Lists are used in numerous passages to organize information and simplify practical guidance. They include five sets of factors by which a commander analyses the strategic balance before war, in Chapter 1 ("Assessing the Conditions"), six categories of terrain enumerated in Chapter 10 ("Terrain"), and five types of intelligence source described in Chapter 13 ("Intelligence Operations"). Each list identifies a class of conflict-related factors or scenarios, and the reader is then offered mental blueprints by which to recognize patterns, set priorities and, where necessary, take action. For example, the list of guidance on tactics to use following an incendiary attack on the enemy position, in Chapter 12 ("Incendiary Attacks"), includes the following rule of thumb: "When a blaze breaks out but the enemy remains calm, wait and watch – do not attack. If practical, follow through as the flames peak. Otherwise stay put" (ch. 12.2).

While classified lists provide structure within individual passages of the text, the work's overall conceptual consistency comes from a set of core strategic ideas. Three of the most powerful of these ideas are conveyed by paired characters carrying opposing meanings: the unconventional and the orthodox, the empty and the solid, and the oblique and the direct. Each of these pairs of complementary opposites opens a new semantic domain in the space between two familiar components. A related effect occurs in English with words like "tragicomic" or "bittersweet", or an oxymoron like "deafening silence" — twin poles of a shared axis. In classical Chinese, where allusion is preferred to direct reference, and fuzzy reasoning trumps raw logic, the use of complementary opposites helps to stretch the imagination, challenging the reader to explore for deeper patterns in the material and grasp abstractions that may be new and unusual.

Key tactical and strategic concepts
The *Sun-tzu* is packed with practical advice for commanders seeking tactical advantage in a range of battlefield and campaign scenarios, but it is the work's strategic dimension that sets it apart.

The message for any would-be all-conquering general is, naturally, to master campaign tactics and mass organizational skills, but also to look beyond those to the task of long-term planning for which he needs a deep understanding of the military and non-military dynamics at play when the interests of different states clash. The general who follows Sun Tzu grounds his approach to these dynamics in hard reality, immune from wishful thinking and emotional reflex. By dint of training and experience, he develops the intuition to recognize and respond to emerging patterns in the overall strategic dynamic. Ultimately he masters that dynamic, reaching beyond conventional formulas to shape a strategic landscape tailored to his objectives.

The tension in the *Sun-tzu* between tactics and strategy, between convention and innovation and between prescribed and improvised responses, is part of a pattern of contrasts at the core of the work, which is highlighted in the following core pairs of complementary opposites.

The unconventional and the orthodox
Qi-zheng (奇正 — "odd/irregular" plus "regular/correct/standard"), in Sun Tzu, is a pair of opposites that alludes to the combination of left-field moves and textbook tactics by which an able commander stays unpredictable.

Until the Warring States era, when the *Sun-tzu* was composed, military convention demanded a degree of honourable conduct on the part of the combatants. It was a fading echo of the chivalric code which, in earlier generations, had governed armed conflict among the nobility of the small principalities and city states of the Yellow River plain. Among other things, that code had precluded acts of outright deviousness in war. By the time of Sun Tzu, however, war had largely transitioned to a new phase of large, attritional campaigns waged without scruple among massive armies directed by technocratic professionals rather than vainglorious aristocrats. Cheating on the rules of war was widespread, though aspects of the old taboos still applied.

Zheng, in the martial context, stood for all that was traditional, correct and proper, in the moral order of the universe as well as in the formations and tactics of the army. *Qi*, by contrast, implied the unpredictable and the unorthodox, in life as in war. Sun Tzu shamelessly celebrates subversive, *qi* approaches ("War is all about trickery and deceit" – ch. 1.5), albeit in a context in which the army and its commanders have first established their *zheng* credentials ("Battles generally begin with orthodox openings, but it is the unconventional move that wins the day" – ch. 5.2). For best results, the *qi* has to stand on a foundation of *zheng*, and vice versa: "Strategic dominance is built on only two types of tactic, the unconventional and the orthodox, but combining them generates more variations than could ever be known." (ch. 5.2).

As the treatise emphasizes, commanders need to remain honourable and upright if they are to inspire confidence and earn the respect of their subordinates. Army hierarchy has to be rigid and efficient, and battalions have to be drilled to perfection in standard formations and maneuvers. These are all *zheng*-type qualities. Yet, according to the Sun Tzu ideal, commanders also have to be masters of subterfuge, cunning and espionage, and the army has to move and fight in a way that is fluid, innovative and wholly unpredictable – all very *qi* concepts. Where necessary, the commander-in-chief is to tear up the rulebook, keeping friends and foes guessing: "Manage the course of battle by adapting to the enemy's approach rather than relying on pre-determined tactics" (ch. 11.11).

So, the pairing of *qi* and *zheng* describes those paradoxically combined approaches – simultaneously novel and traditional, honourable and devious, orthodox and unconventional – that a gifted and experienced Sun Tzu-type commander brings to war, at both the tactical and strategic levels.

The empty and the solid

Xu-shi (虛實 – "empty/immaterial" plus "substantive/solid"), in Sun Tzu, indicates the asymmetrical presence or absence of military forces at a given locale, by which a commander ensures he has overwhelming numerical superiority at the point of combat: "When troops take action, the impact must be that of a whetstone flung against an egg. It is a matter of asymmetrical force" (ch. 5.1).

Rather than going head-to-head against enemies of similar or greater strength, the able commander aims to act unopposed, maneuvering to concentrate his elite or massed forces against weak points where enemy soldiers are absent, or thin on the ground, or are rendered ineffective by sickness, poor leadership or lack of weapons: "To advance without being repulsed, thrust where opposing forces are most dispersed" (ch. 6.3). Meanwhile, he lures the enemy's best forces to expend their energy striking at shadows, and ensures that the enemy's lesser units, if they attack, encounter fierce resistance from a well-prepared mass of defenders, properly led and full of zeal:

"An accomplished campaigner imposes his will on the

34

opponent rather than being imposed upon. He entices the enemy to move of his own accord into the intended position. He deters the enemy from going where he would otherwise go" (ch. 6.1).

Mastery of the *xu-shi* principle means exploiting the opportunities for tactical and strategic advantage that fluctuate, as fluidly as water, between *xu* and *shi*: "Water forms channels according to the lie of the land, and armies fashion victory according to the presence of the enemy" (ch. 6.7).

The oblique and the direct
Yu-zhi (迂直 — "winding/circuitous" plus "straight/direct"), in Sun Tzu, refers to the guileful interplay of linear and non-linear movements by which a commander misdirects the enemy, while his own forces maneuver for initiative.

At an operational level, the commander applies his mastery of this principle to delay and exhaust the enemy in the run-up to battle:

"By side-tracking the opponent and distracting him with easy gains, one reaches the battlefield first despite marching later" (ch. 7.1).

At the more strategic and philosophical levels, the commander must correctly assess the benefits of taking direct action in pursuit of a military objective, compared with those of holding off or adopting a more circuitous approach: "Weigh up the strategic benefits before making a move. The commander who best masters the interplay between oblique and direct maneuvers, will prevail" (ch. 7.3).

As with *qi-zheng* (unconventional/orthodox) and *xu-shi* (empty/solid), the *yu-zhi* (winding/straight) pairing works in both a literal and figurative sense. The enemy must be physically misdirected on the ground and mentally wrong-footed in his planning and preparations, in both cases expending valuable energy and resources before battle. And in common with those other pairings, the *yu-zhi* principle instils in readers a tactical and strategic approach that emphasizes mind and maneuvers over brute force.

These three key pairs of complementary opposites in Sun Tzu form part of a pattern of dual perspectives that permeates the treatise. Each, in its way, reproduces the tension between chaos and order that is fundamental to military action.

Order is the conventional military solution to the chaos of the fight. Hierarchies are established, discipline is imposed and maneuvers are drilled, Formations are fixed and tactics are developed and honed. Lines, columns and squares are used to concentrate manpower into manageable, moving blocks, controlled through a strict regimen of command. The larger the military machine, the greater the reliance on organized systems of management and control.

But as the scale of armies expanded during the Warring States era, it was discovered that too much order in the structure of an army or the planning of a campaign hardened into brittleness and inertia. A rigid, rectilinear force can be outflanked by one that is more flexibly configured. Orthodox tactics may be rendered defunct by an opponent's unanticipated gambit. A cautious, deliberative commander may be stunned by the audacity of a faster-thinking, more innovative rival.

The tactical and strategic guidance in the *Sun-tzu* plays repeatedly on this paradox. To seize victory in the fog of war, the commander needs a measure of order and control on his side, while imposing disorder and uncertainty on his opponent.

"Disorder on one side comes from order on the other" (ch. 5.4). Yet he needs to remain seemingly chaotic enough to disrupt the ordered plans and fixed formations of the opposition, such that "the enemy does not know where to defend [and] does not know where to attack" (ch. 6.2).

For the Sun Tzu commander, there are three grounding concepts by which to navigate the resulting jumble of possibilities. The first is "victory" itself. The sovereign and his chief commander must clarify their conception of success, whether for a one-off battle or a lengthy campaign. What will victory look like? How will it be measured? What happens afterwards? The second is "knowledge". The decisions they make and the actions they take in pursuit of victory, need to be grounded in concrete reality, as understood via the objective assessment of verifiable facts. The third is a specialist concept particular to Sun Tzu, which is translated here mostly as "strategic dominance" (*shi*, 勢). The astute commander looks beyond immediate appearances to the shifting currents, or patterns of forces, that underlie every aspect of the conflict. To the degree that it is possible, he works to shape those currents for advantage, and ultimately to gain such an overwhelming advantage that the outcome of the conflict becomes a foregone conclusion.

Victory

It is asserted from the outset in the *Sun-tzu* that victory is the sole standard against which a commander benchmarks his decisions, actions, tactics and strategic considerations in the run-up to and during armed conflict. Not glory, reputation, pride, popularity, morality or political expedience—those are auxiliary or irrelevant. The objective is to win, not just to fight. What matters is to suppress or eliminate the threat that an adversary poses to one's own state, and that goal may be achieved either bloodlessly or by battle, depending on the circumstances. Sun Tzu is clear about which is better: "The military ideal is to force an opposing army to submit without battle" (ch. 3.1).

It is worth noting the contrast between the ideal of victory without destruction advocated by Sun Tzu, and the focus in Clausewitz, the West's nearest equivalent in influence, on victory as the culmination of a process in which both sides inevitably escalate towards maximum available force in the effort to destroy one another. Indeed, Clausewitz, in his book *On War*, dismissed the idea of victory without battle as nonsense. For Sun Tzu, however, battle is such a risky and costly component of the campaign to achieve state objectives that it is much better if a lower-risk, lower-cost alternative can be found. This explains why the "best tacticians of old" (ch. 4.2), often faded invisibly into history. Their victories were such battle-free walkovers that they failed to leave a trail of corpses and devastation in their wake.

The twin objectives of victory without bloodshed where possible, and a coup de grace delivered on the battlefield where necessary, are pursued in parallel throughout the *Sun-tzu*. But in both cases, the commander must also grasp the point that victory, whether bloody or otherwise, is of limited worth if it simply seeds the ground for another costly phase of conflict: "No state has ever profited from protracted war" (ch. 2.2).

Knowledge

Any commander applying principles from Sun Tzu, having set his sights on victory, must then assess the factors that may influence that outcome. Rational analysis is emphasized in the treatise as a source of reliable knowledge, and knowledge is key to the Sun Tzu commander's success. Indeed, the treatise begins and ends with chapters on the practical aspects of gathering accurate information by which to assess and influence the course of the conflict.

Chapter 1 opens with a five-part methodology for compiling and assessing comparative data on the two sides, while Chapter 13 stresses that judiciously managed intelligence operations provide the only assurance of anticipating an enemy's intentions.

As the intervening chapters make clear, knowing everything about the enemy it is not, in itself, enough. A successful commander must also thoroughly understand conditions on his own side, including the capacity, morale and readiness of his troops, as well as being able to objectively appraise his own personal and professional capabilities.

"When a commander understands equally well the condition of the opposition and the condition of his own side, his victory is never in doubt" (ch. 10.5).

Sun Tzu also counsels commanders to obtain in-depth information about the terrain that must be marched, and about the battleground itself, so as to smooth progress and multiply their tactical options.

"The best generals assess the challenges of the terrain and plan for the distances involved, so as to anticipate the enemy and create conditions for victory"(ch. 10.3).

Knowledge, in the *Sun-tzu*, is acquired partly in the form of empirically derived information, partly by correct analysis of that information, partly through studious preparation – the statement "It is imperative that this be studied and understood in depth" occurs five times in the treatise – and partly as a matter of judgment and experience. It is by developing his ability to acquire knowledge and objectively appraise conditions, at the operational level and in the broader strategic environment, that the Sun Tzu commander nurtures the awareness he needs to impose a necessary degree of order on the chaos of conflict.

Strategic dominance
A clear conception of victory and a solid foundation of objective knowledge together give the commander a sound footing for analysing and understanding the position he finds himself in at

any point during the conflict. In order to anticipate the position he is likely to be in tomorrow, or next month, however, he needs also to comprehend the evolving flow of events in which both he, and his adversary, are key actors. Better still, he needs to take command of that flow of events and turn it to advantage. This is where the concept of *shi* (勢) comes into play.

"Strategic dominance," as *shi* is rendered in this translation, refers to the inexorable momentum, both operational and strategic, that one side acquires when the balance of military tension tips irreversibly in its favour. Sun Tzu offers vivid analogies for this phenomenon. Strategic dominance is "like a torrent, forceful enough to tumble boulders" (ch. 5.3). Gaining strategic dominance is "like drawing taut a crossbow," (ch. 5.3). And, "For the commander who successfully exploits strategic dominance, giving battle is akin to rolling logs and boulders down a slope" (ch. 5.5).

The astute commander is always watching for trends and patterns among the factors that drive the strategic dynamic. Chapter 1 of the treatise groups these factors into five sets, some determined by the tactical and strategic choices of the commander himself, some dependent on the political and military institutions of the state, and some environmental, such as weather conditions and terrain. The balance among them continually shifts, sometimes subtly and sometimes dramatically. The Sun Tzu commander, who recognizes that he cannot simply impose static order on a dynamic situation, endeavours to read the currents and steer events in his side's favour: "Strategic dominance is a matter of exercising control over the situation by exploiting opportunities" (ch. 1.4).

"Victory", "knowledge" and "strategic dominance" are foundational concepts in Sun Tzu, along with the treatise's three core pairs of complementary opposites. Together they orient readers towards what is probably the most fundamental skill of Sun Tzu-style military command — the ability to discern and act on deep patterns identified among the complex conditions of war. A useful way to contextualize these concepts, and the holistic science of war that they give rise to, is to briefly consider the dominant philosophical currents of the Warring States era.

Philosophical backdrop
An early task of Chinese philosophical thinking was to intuit deep patterns in the imagined workings of the universe, based on the rhythms in Nature that governed the lives of people in a settled, agrarian society. The methodological approach was largely holistic, seeking to relate the local to the global and the global to the local. For example, by observing natural phenomena like the flow of a stream, the phases of the moon and the cycle of life, death and renewal, one might infer cosmic principles based on currents and cycles, which could in turn inform an understanding of human affairs. In their holistic approach, Chinese philosophies differed from the methods of reductionist reasoning — analysing problems by dissecting them into their smallest constituent elements — that were coming to prevail in the Mediterranean region during that same period. Thinkers in ancient China attached greater value to ideas that conformed with direct experience and could be conveyed by analogy, than to knowledge based on an accumulation of logically linked facts.

Just as in ancient Greece, there was to begin with no sharp distinction in the Warring States world between applied knowledge and pure philosophy. The philosophical theories that endured in ancient China were those that could best be put to practical use in the realms of statecraft, medicine, ethics, military affairs and human relations. Practitioners in each of these fields shared a common recognition that the world and its diverse phenomena were subject to endless flux, some of it proceeding according to pattern and some of it incomprehensible. For example, the observation that extremes tended to be followed by reversals had the force of universal law. One way or another, good times would be followed by bad times, and then by good times again, and so on. Similarly with the observation that things that were joined together tended to break up, and later to merge again, and later still to break up again. Allies would at some point become enemies, and enemies would at some point become allies.

Whether or not there was a purpose to all this flux, or an ideal state into which conditions might eventually subside, was another matter, and not a particularly practical one. The point was to recognize the inevitability of change, and come to know some of its patterns, and then, to the degree that one had personal control, to navigate a pathway through evolving circumstances in a manner that delivered a desired outcome – which might be a good harvest, moral virtue, political success, social harmony, or military victory.

That pathway was called the *dao* (道), literally a road or a way, and by implication the right road or way. Over the centuries the concept of *dao* became progressively more abstract and esoteric, as the practice of philosophy branched beyond its practical origins. In Warring States China, however, to write of the *dao* in any given field of knowledge was, in general, to apply a functional concept.

The Warring States era was philosophically eclectic, with numerous schools of thought attracting adherents and competing for patronage. All shared a fundamental faith in the principle of flux, and each employed, in their respective fashion, the trope of the *dao*. The different schools were, during this period, in the process of coalescing into the three broad ideologies that later came to be established as Taoism, Confucianism and Legalism, and traces of each can be found in the *Sun-tzu*.

Taoism

The earliest Taoist thinkers, before "Taoism" took shape as a discrete body of beliefs, were naturalists, astrologists and alchemists. They classified and interpreted natural phenomena, and aimed to apply their knowledge of Nature's workings for human ends. The mental frameworks they developed included the Yin-Yang model of complementary opposites (such as darkness and light, heat and cold, male and female), the Five Elements system of classification (which depicted all the world and its affairs in terms of interactions among water, fire, wood, metal and soil), and various methods of arithmetical divination (based on observation of particular natural phenomena under controlled conditions). There was an occultist aspect to these approaches, but they also formed the origins of the scientific outlook, in China as in the West.

The embryonic science of war set out in the *Sun-tzu* draws heavily on those proto-Taoist models in order to analyse — and propose ways of mastering — the challenges of interstate conflict. For example, a number of core concepts in the treatise are conveyed in the paradoxical, Yin-Yang idiom of complementary opposites. Much of the advice in the treatise is structured into five-part methodologies and systems of classification. Arithmetical calculation is asserted as the basis for comparative assessment of strategic strength ahead of battle. And metaphors from Nature are frequently invoked to suggest how the balance of forces mutates and shifts during war.

There is also the pervading emphasis on avoiding unnecessary death and damage during a military campaign, to the opposition as well as to one's own side. This brings practical benefits in terms of conserving resources and averting a cycle of destruction. But it also chimes with the Taoist faith in life as the highest value in the living world, and in Nature as the ultimate arbiter of what is right in human affairs.

The presiding spirit behind the *Sun-tzu* clearly identified with the Taoist insight that while it is futile to try and impose complete control over a naturally chaotic and unpredictable flow of events, a measure of systematic control is nevertheless achievable. And in a complex, organic system like war, the best results come from applying a holistic, grand-strategy perspective, and working with, rather than across, the grain of that system's inherent trends.

Confucianism

The conceptual approaches of the proto-Taoists eventually merged into what became known as Taoism, and this was partly a reaction to the emergence and establishment of Confucianism as state dogma during China's early imperial era.

The teachings of Confucius (551–479 BC) had emphasized people's hierarchical obligations to one another as members of a family and of wider society, in line with venerable traditions and a rigid code of ethics. During the Warring States period, Confucius's disciples and followers expanded on the theme of moral virtue as a society's central organizing principle, within a structure of precisely graded hierarchies, and they came to dominate the school of "literati" – the scholars and tutors who instructed the offspring of the nobility and advised them in their political careers. Their debates were an essential element in the philosophical backdrop of the era in which the *Sun-tzu* emerged.

Unlike the Taoists, for whom worldly problems manifested the error of civilization's departure from the natural *dao* of the universe, Confucius's followers attributed society's ills to loss of moral *dao*. Accordingly, they asserted that political and social harmony should be restored by imposition of moral order, maintained through a hierarchy of patriarchal relationships and a system of sacred rites, dating from a distant, golden age. Where the archetypal Taoist had been a recluse, shunning society so as to commune with Nature, the archetypal Confucian was a political busybody, prescribing correct conduct for rulers and ruled alike.

Confucianism eventually became the guiding creed of the Chinese imperium, encouraged by emperors and officials who were drawn to the vision of a pyramidal society of harmony and virtue, headed by a caste of enlightened royals and structured around a moral and social order that was conservative, rational and humane. In contrast, the amoral strictures of Sun Tzu were anathema, and for many centuries the treatise was stigmatized. By seeming to welcome the cunning and deception of the military campaign into the non-military realms of government and interstate relations, the *Sun-tzu* was thought to undermine the moral foundations of the world-under-heaven.

Legalism

The third — and most influential — ideology to coalesce during the Warring States era, was the "rules-based governance" school of thought, known in English as Legalism because of its association with an excessively harsh and inflexible penal code.

Legalism, in which the principles of bureaucratic administration in a mass-population state first began to be codified, developed symbiotically with the science of military organization during the Warring States period, and in fact was inspired by practices and insights first developed in the military context. The mass army under a Sun Tzu-type regimen of discipline and control was in many ways the archetype for the perfect Legalist state. Legalism reduced the complex challenge of governing mass populations of chaotically interacting individuals and groups to the relative clarity and order of army command. Everyone beneath the level of the ruler would be subject to the same impartial system of penalties and rewards, ruthlessly enforced by means of mutual surveillance, with the threat of collective punishment for individual lapses. Universal standardization and regimented predictability were imposed to stamp out organic messiness.

It was no accident, therefore, that the intellectual home and proving ground of Legalism was the kingdom of Qin, the most avowedly militarist of the warring states. Qin went on to conquer all its rivals and then briefly established the prototype for subsequent East Asian empires: a regime that was highly centralized and bureaucratic; rigid and unforgiving in the implementation of a strict, top-down legal code; and with a fetish for uniformity and standardization. As things turned out, the Qin edifice rapidly imploded under the tensions of its own inflexible logic, and Legalism's cruel excesses were rejected under the more humane regime that eventually took its place. However, Legalism of a less extreme form has remained the governing principle of the Chinese state ever since, and in fact its influence is present in the centralizing, regulatory tendencies of every modern nation-state.

Theorists of Legalism particularly promoted the concept of *shi* (勢), or "potency" (which appears in Sun Tzu as "strategic dominance") to describe the irresistible authority by which an infallible ruler imposes his will through his ministers into the bureaucracy and out across the whole of society. Legalism was, in other words, a philosophy of pure power, anti-Nature and amoral to the core, even though several of its founding concepts had been drawn from the Taoist and Confucian traditions. From the Legalist perspective, the Taoist ideal of intuitive, light-touch government, was dangerous and naïve in an era of vast, complex societies geared for perpetual warfare, while Confucian morality was simply an irrelevance as soon as it presented any kind of obstacle to the supreme authority of the sovereign and his mission of ruling an internally strong, militarily powerful state.

The notion of flux was as implicit in Legalism as it was in the other main schools of thought of the classical era, but the *dao* that Legalists offered in response was the road towards a tightly regimented, rationally organized state run by a strong, impersonal government under an all-powerful ruler.

In their early, Warring-States incarnations, Taoism, Confucianism and Legalism each acknowledged the reciprocity between chaos and order, and each theorized ways for society and individuals to operate in the fluctuating space between those poles. The Taoists sought to balance civilization with Nature, and looked for models within the ineffable cosmic order that was presumed to guide Nature. Confucianism offered an ideal of harmony sustained by moral self-restraint and a rigid social and familial hierarchy. Legalism advocated consciously imposed order, in the form of strictly administered, top-down systems for command and control. Each of those approaches left its mark on the *Sun-tzu*, in which war is depicted as a realm of barely comprehensible chaos in which the astute commander marks out the necessary modicum of military, political and moral order to achieve his goal, but not so much as to trigger blowback in the form of fierce resistance or reversal.

In structure and content, the *Sun-tzu* offered its early readers a practical toolkit. It provided a functional compilation of tactical and strategic guidance, presented in a coherent framework of theory and grounded on familiar philosophical footings. And it outlined the world's first, embryonic science of war for an emerging class of military professionals keen to make sense of and exploit developments in their fast-evolving field.

The methodical, systematic nature of the treatise has been obscured in English by a reluctance to associate Sun Tzu's holistic perspective with the notion of "science," along with a tendency to regard the work as a jumbled repository of aphorisms, mundane in places and mystical in others. In translation it has been presented as a scrapbook disquisition on the wise, old, Oriental "art" of warfare. This was in part a misreading of the structured unity of the text, and in part the result of misunderstandings about the relationship between orally transmitted teachings and the manuscripts into which they were collated around 2,300 years ago, when disseminating philosophical ideas in written form was still a novelty.

In the chapters of this translation of the *Sun-tzu*, we may now find, as its early readers did, a systematically presented body of applied military knowledge, based on a holistic, grand-strategy approach that extends well beyond the clash of arms itself.

3
Can a commander win the Sun Tzu way?

This section explores Sun Tzu's practical influence on warfare by examining the careers of three giants of military history: Cao Cao (155-220), Genghis Khan (c. 1167-1227) and Napoleon (1769-1821), all of whom either did or could have had access to the *Sun-tzu* as they planned and ran their military campaigns.

Each of the three was a master tactician who excelled in military organization, mental cunning and rapid maneuver, and they all had a habit of unbalancing opponents who enjoyed the advantage of home territory or troop numbers, but who were hampered by their own relatively conventional thinking and predictable movements. Just as with Sun Wu and Sun Bin in the period when the *Sun-tzu* first coalesced, each of the three tended to out-scheme the opposition well before battle, at a strategic level that their enemies were barely aware existed.

Sun Wu reputedly guided the kingdom of Wu to conquer the larger and more powerful Kingdom of Chu in 506 BC in a campaign which marked the birth in ancient China of long-range, multi-battle strategy. One-and-a-half centuries later, his notional descendant Sun Bin combined rigid military discipline with a capacity for battlefield flexibility and brilliantly executed tactical ruses in a form which came to be encapsulated in — and forever associated with — the *Sun-tzu*. The two Suns may have pioneered the Sun Tzu "science of war," but it was several centuries before the emergence of the first of the greatest Sun Tzu practitioners, the commanders who came closest to "fight[ing] a hundred battles without ever facing defeat" (ch. 3.7).

Cao Cao

The short-lived Qin dynasty (221–206 BC) which established China's first empire, was succeeded, after a brief interlude, by four centuries of consolidation under the Han dynasty (206 BC–AD 220). Towards the end of that period, imperial authority crumbled and civil war raged. Foremost among the regional warlords battling to control the throne, was the scholar-warlord Cao Cao, who authored the earliest known commentary on the *Sun-tzu* and was steeped in the treatise's tactical and strategic approaches.

First commentary

In his preface to the commentary, believed to have been written early in his career, Cao wrote:

> I have read plenty of volumes on military matters and battlefield tactics, among which Sun Wu's is the most profound....It cannot be faulted in its detailed attention to assessing conditions ahead of battle, its emphasis on military mobilization, its clarity of strategic conception and its depth of tactical design. Our contemporaries, however, have failed to truly grasp the substance of its teachings, and while implementing many of the lesser points they miss the main thrust.

Judging by the annotations that make up Cao's commentary, along with his subsequent military exploits, we may infer that the "main thrust" he sought to elaborate was related to the balance that a commander must strike between strategic conception and operational tactics. He has to master the strategic landscape before risking his army in battle, and for this he needs to understand, influence and exploit the wider pattern of factors connected with conflict, including any economic, political, environmental and psychological factors that have a bearing on the eventual outcome.

Smart tactics are essential, too, but are pointless if not consistent with a larger strategic design. Sun Tzu emphasizes, for example, that the costs of military action are always heavy and often devastating, even for the victor, and the types of tactics or personalities that propel countries into military action without proper regard for the strategic consequences, are therefore to be strictly guarded against.

As Cao notes in his preface:

> The astute leader's principle in military matters is to keep his forces in check, moving when the occasion requires. He takes military action only when there is no alternative.

Cao reiterates this "only when there is no alternative" caveat throughout his commentary, as if channelling Sun Tzu's assertion that "the military ideal is to force an opposing army to submit without battle" (ch. 3.1). Cao did indeed pick his fights with caution, and prepared for them carefully, yet he was revered for tactical flair, military discipline and uncanny speed (to this day his name is idiomatic in Chinese for that talk-of-the-devil moment when someone turns up just as they are being talked about), and if anything he built his career — and eventually a new dynasty — on precipitating rather than avoiding military action.

Characteristic victories
In each of his three most significant victories, Cao employed an unexpected, oblique approach, in the Sun Tzu manner, against an enemy braced for a more conventional, head-on assault.

In AD 200 , Cao achieved the defining victory of his career, against Yuan Shao, the then-dominant warlord, who was based north of the Yellow River in what is now Hebei province. Yuan Shao, expecting to crush the upstart general, had advanced

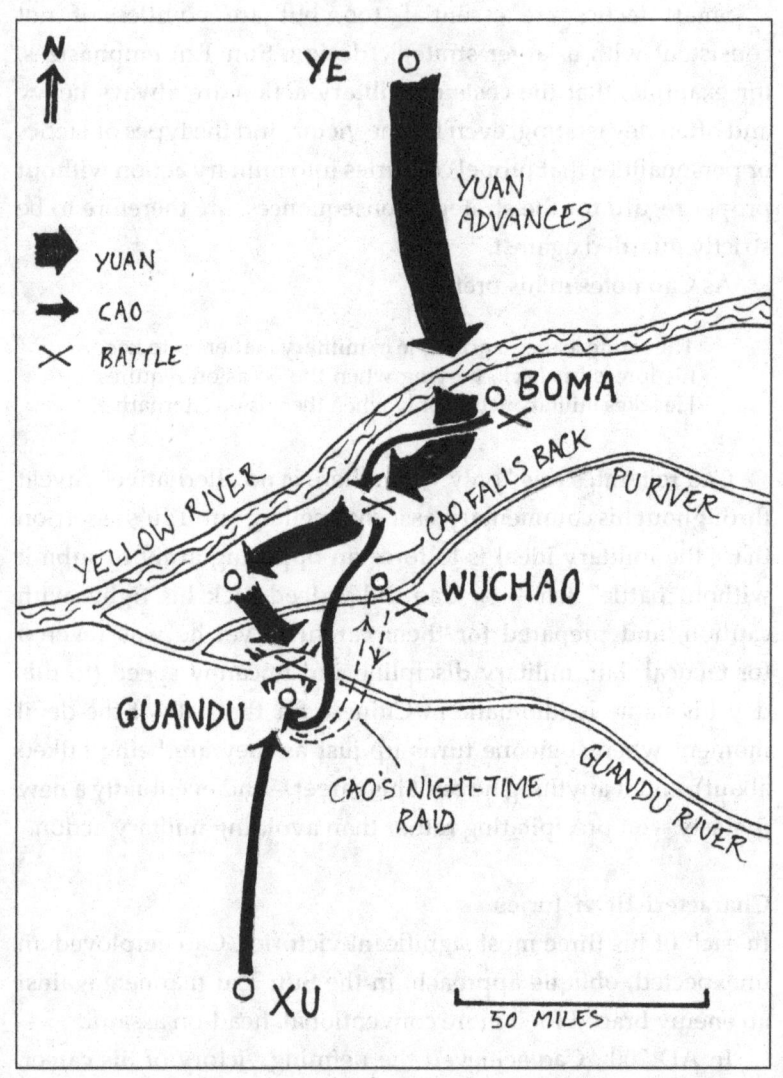

Map 3

Cao Cao at the battle of Guandu, AD 200

Cao Cao and Yuan Shao, the dominant warlords of Northern China as the Han dynasty crumbled, were on collision course despite being separated by the Yellow River. Yuan despatched his army of 110,000 across the River early in AD 200, and began a cautious advance towards Cao's capital at Xu (now Xuchang City in Henan province). Wary of the superior mobility of Cao's far smaller forces on home territory, Yuan opted to keep his huge army together.

At Guandu, Cao had a line of defensive earthworks ready, and the two sides dug in for an attritional stalemate lasting months. As winter approached, Cao's position became precarious. Supplies were low and he had fewer than 10,000 men at his disposal. But Yuan's advantage was fragile. Defectors from Yuan's high command gave Cao vital intelligence on the huge army's over-extended supply lines, and Cao was able to destroy Yuan's main stock of provisions and materiel, at the town of Wuchao, in a daring night-time incendiary raid.

With winter looming and no time to re-provision, Yuan immediately launched a head-on assault against the defenders at Guandu. But his men were unnerved by the news from Wuchao, the assault failed, and Yuan's army was routed. Cao drove Yuan all the way back to and across the Yellow River—only around 800 of his men escaped across the river with him. Yuan and his sons fought on for another few years, but never again gained the upper hand over Cao.

south across the Yellow River onto territory governed by Cao, steadily securing supply lines for his army of over 100,000 men. Cao's smaller forces conducted a fighting retreat, steering the invaders towards a specially prepared battle zone close to Guandu, in today's Henan province, where the terrain favoured the defenders. As expected, Yuan's battalions slowed to a halt and both sides began to fortify along a frontline stretching for many miles. While Yuan's forces were preparing for their final offensive, Cao's cavalry destroyed their two main supply depots in raids to the east and west, thus depriving the vast army of provisions and equipment just as winter was approaching. His hand forced, Yuan promptly launched a frontal assault on the defenders at Guandu, which failed, and his army withdrew in disarray. Cao's main forces emerged from behind their fortifications and pursued Yuan's broken army back across the Yellow River, establishing Cao Cao as the most powerful figure in northern China.

To the northeast of his nascent kingdom, in AD 207, in what is now Liaoning province, Cao outflanked the defending forces of the Wuhuan confederation, leading his army on an arduous detour through mountains to the north of his objective rather than waiting for floodwaters to subside from the direct route along the coastal strip, as expected. Cao's army had spent months constructing a series of canals specifically to supply an offensive along the southern route, so the Wuhuan were caught off-guard by Cao's sudden appearance on high ground to their north, and they collected in alarm only to be routed at White Wolf Mountain (Bailang Shan, 白狼山), near the present-day city of Lingyuan.

Then in AD 211, Cao subdued an alliance of his adversaries at Huayin (near the confluence of the Wei and Yellow Rivers in today's Shaanxi province) after a similarly audacious flanking maneuver, despatching his army on a roundabout route via three major river crossings, so as to emerge at the rear of the alliance's original defensive position. By his own account he then compounded the confusion among his opponents by feigning weakness and settling in for a period of protracted peace negotiations, before splintering them with a sudden attack.

The victory at Huayin illustrates Cao's reputation for deviousness, for which he came to be stigmatized in the historical record, and there is no denying that trickery and deception were as core to Cao's military approach, as they are to the strategy and tactics advocated by Sun Tzu. Earlier in Cao's career, at Anzhong (near Nanyang in today's Henan province) in AD 198, instinctive cunning helped him save his army from a nearly hopeless position, trapped in a steep valley with pursuers closing in and the exit route ahead blocked by more foes. During the night, Cao had his men dig an entrenchment along the side of the valley, where he concealed a contingent of troops. At dawn, his baggage train was seen taking to the road amid signs of panic, and the enemy renewed the chase, scenting victory. The concealed contingent fell on the enemy's rear as it passed by, while the main body of Cao's troops turned and attacked their pursuers head on. The enemy were thrown into confusion and annihilated. As Cao said later, invoking Sun Tzu terminology: "They decided to check my army mid-retreat and make me give battle in the fight-to-the-death zone. Consequently I knew what we had to do to triumph."

Machiavellian reputation
Cao's penchant for cunning was anathema to the conservative, right-thinking Confucian moralists of later generations in China, as were Sun Tzu's glorification of subterfuge and spying. Consequently, both Sun Tzu and Cao Cao have been tainted, throughout Chinese history, with a reputation for (in European

terms) Machiavellian amorality.

It is true that Cao, in his commentary, highlights with apparent approval the devious approaches to war advocated by Sun Tzu. Advice, for example, to apply underhand measures wherever appropriate, to unbalance the enemy by asymmetrical concentrations of force, to blend conventional and unexpected tactics in an unpredictable way, to err on the side of secrecy and subtlety over assertiveness and brute force, and for the chief commander to devote much of his time and energy to espionage.

Yet Cao's commentary shows that he also valued Sun Tzu's more orthodox insistence on clearly defined military and political goals, objective collection and analysis of information, rigorous planning and logistics, and the need to calculate full costs before resorting to military action.

Cao was prickly and ruthless, but he accepted constructive criticism and had a habit of attracting and retaining the loyalty of capable officers and officials, many of whom had defected from his foes. (Sun Tzu identifies defectors and turned spies as particularly valuable sources of intelligence.) With their help he battled his way to supremacy among the warlords of the day, meanwhile bringing civil administration and economic stability to the lands under his control amid the decades-long turmoil at the close of the Han dynasty.

It was perhaps in this respect, above all, that Cao Cao approximated to the Sun Tzu ideal of the successful, far-sighted commander: strict, methodical, brave, dependable, and attentive to the welfare of the troops and civilians under his command.

Genghis Khan

A millennium later, another military leader fighting the Sun Tzu way stormed across northern China, sacking cities en route to founding a new imperial dynasty. China was just one conquest among many for Genghis Khan and his Mongol armies, but it was by far the most significant in terms of influence on Mongol strategy and tactics. The Sun Tzu approach to mass, organized combat, which the Mongols adopted in part from China, brought them a stunning record of military success and revolutionized the way that war was fought all across the Eurasian landmass.

Genghis the man

As a man, Genghis Khan was strict, ascetic and tough. He rode and fought alongside his Mongol fighters into his mid-sixties, never asking them to die for him and always strategizing to ensure overwhelming local advantage before committing them to battle. And for this he retained their devotion throughout his life.

Similar to Cao Cao, Genghis was ruthless towards those who crossed him but he was otherwise controlled and methodical in his approach to outwitting and overwhelming his enemies. Like Cao, he had the natural leader's knack for inspiring loyalty, neutralizing rivals, and rallying competing groups to his cause. He had a questing mind, and sought out wisdom and advice from the scholars, philosophers, astronomers, and religious figures in the territories he conquered.

His armies inspired terror by the speed and ferocity of their assaults, and people were slaughtered by the tens of thousands in each of his major campaigns, but Genghis, by the standards of the day, was no despot. In fact, during an era of feudal tyranny and arbitrary aristocratic rule, he turned out to be a progressive lawgiver, abolishing torture in lands that submitted to his rule, granting religious freedom and bringing safer trade routes, lighter taxes and universal male education. As Geoffrey Chaucer's squire reports of Genghis in *The Canterbury Tales*:

> There was nowhere in the wide world known
> So excellent a lord in everything.

Rise to power

When Temüjin, as he was originally named, first emerged as a young chieftain, the Mongols were just one among several loose-knit tribal groupings spread across the steppes and forests of central Asia. Several decades earlier, one of those groupings, the semi-nomadic Jurchen—who were the Mongols' traditional overlords—had fought their way into Northern China and seized control, and were now settled there as rulers over a population of thirty or forty million Chinese farmers and town-dwellers.

Partly due to his martial instincts, partly through good fortune, and partly by charisma and determination, Genghis prevailed through a succession of inter-clan power struggles and began to attract allegiance from other groupings on the steppes. By 1206 his confederation of grassland tribes, united under Mongol banners, was formidable enough to challenge the Jurchen for a share of the spoils of ruling northern China, which remained vulnerable to attack by nomad raiders despite being the world's richest and most technologically-advanced society.

Rather than taking on the Jurchen directly, Genghis initially chose to attack the kingdom of the Tanguts, a wealthy vassal state of the Jurchen occupying a swathe of what is now western China, separated from the Mongol heartland by the Gobi desert.

The nomads' advantage in any conflict with the farmers to their south, lay in speed and mobility. Every warrior in their all-cavalry armies was schooled from childhood in the skills of horseback fighting, including rapid attack and retreat, and in battle they worked together with the discipline and cohesion innate to their way of life as hunters and herders on the steppes.

The mostly infantry armies of the Chinese and of the Tanguts were by comparison better armoured and better regimented, but their movements were relatively slow and predictable. And whereas each of the nomad warriors was a willing combatant, an expert bowman or lancer and strongly motivated by the prospect of booty, the typical Chinese or Tangut soldier was a reluctant and poorly-trained conscript.

In an escalating series of raids into Tangut territory, from 1207 to 1209, the Mongols closed in on the capital, Yinchuan, until they found themselves blocked at a heavily-defended mountain pass guarding the final approach to the city. Unable to break through, the Mongols feigned partial retreat and, using a standard tactic of the steppes, baited the defenders out onto the plain where they were easily cut down by Genghis's swiftly returning cavalry.

The Mongols then laid siege to Yinchuan, but lacking the equipment and expertise for siege warfare, they were stumped. In a bungled attempt to undermine the defenders by breaking dykes to inundate the city, the Mongols managed to flood themselves out of their own camp and destroy crops in the surrounding farmland that they were due to rely on for sustenance. The resulting stalemate was concluded with an agreement: the Tanguts agreed to transfer allegiance from the Jurchen to the Mongols and supply them with booty and livestock, and in return, Genghis withdrew his army.

Newly emboldened by the rewards of the Tangut campaign, the Mongols turned their full attention to the Jurchen. They launched their first offensive in 1211 and besieged the capital at

Zhongdu, on the site of today's Beijing, on and off for several years until it capitulated in 1215. Once again, having seized all the gold and silk they could transport, the Mongol army headed back towards their homeland, Genghis having no interest, at that point, in taking control over an alien, sedentary population.

Learning from China
There was little in the faltering campaign against the Tanguts, or the attritional assault on Zhongdu and other northern Chinese cities to suggest that the Mongols were on their way to founding a sprawling cross-continental empire. But Zhongdu marked a significant development.

Bands of nomadic herdsmen had been attacking farming settlements along the plains of the Yellow River for two thousand years, but none had previously besieged and sacked a major walled city. What the Mongols demonstrated at Zhongdu was that they could combine the strengths of a disciplined, determined, tightly coordinated raiding party fresh from the steppes, with China's centuries-long experience in the science of mass military organization—which Genghis and his fellow grasslands commanders were acquiring through their struggles with the sinicized Tanguts and Jurchen, as well as directly from military and administrative specialists among the Mongols' growing number of Chinese captives and defectors.

Genghis's early battles in the internecine steppe wars had involved at most a few thousand riders on each side, but now he and his generals headed armies of tens of thousands of men, and faced organizational problems similar to those analysed by Sun Tzu.

Like Cao Cao long before him, Genghis established firm control of his armies by imposing fierce discipline, training and preparation. Cao had ensured that senior officers were appointed on the basis of skill and experience rather than social rank or family connections, and as a result they were loyal to him and the system he had created, rather than to their personal patrons. Cao could also rely on the dedication of soldier-farmers settled in the military agricultural colonies established by him in areas denuded by years of civil war.

A thousand years later, Genghis introduced a similar, Chinese-style system of military governance to steppe society, organizing the tribal population into a regimental structure and compelling each family to supply men for mixed-clan army units of ten, 100, 1,000 and 10,000 troops. Like Cao, Genghis recruited according to talent rather than connections, and many of his best men were commoners elevated by him into positions of command, and fiercely loyal to him as a result.

After the sacking of Zhongdu, Genghis began to look westwards, and during the last decade of his life, from 1217 to 1227, he and his generals conquered a succession of powerful, well-armed empires and kingdoms along the trade routes of central Asia, extending deep into Persia and the principalities of Russia. His sons and grandsons took up the baton after his death, crushing opposition as far as Syria and Poland, as well as eventually occupying and ruling the whole of China.

In the field, the Mongols applied the full panoply of traditional grassland stratagems, though on a scale that was orders of magnitude greater than anything seen previously. The three-pronged pincer attack executed with speed and precision; the feigned retreat followed by lightning-fast reversal; and the stealthy, swift encirclement heralding a hail of arrows from every direction. The Mongols' highly trained cavalry armies operated to a general plan of action jointly determined by Genghis and his generals but were otherwise autonomous and self-sufficient during a campaign, with their commanders in constant

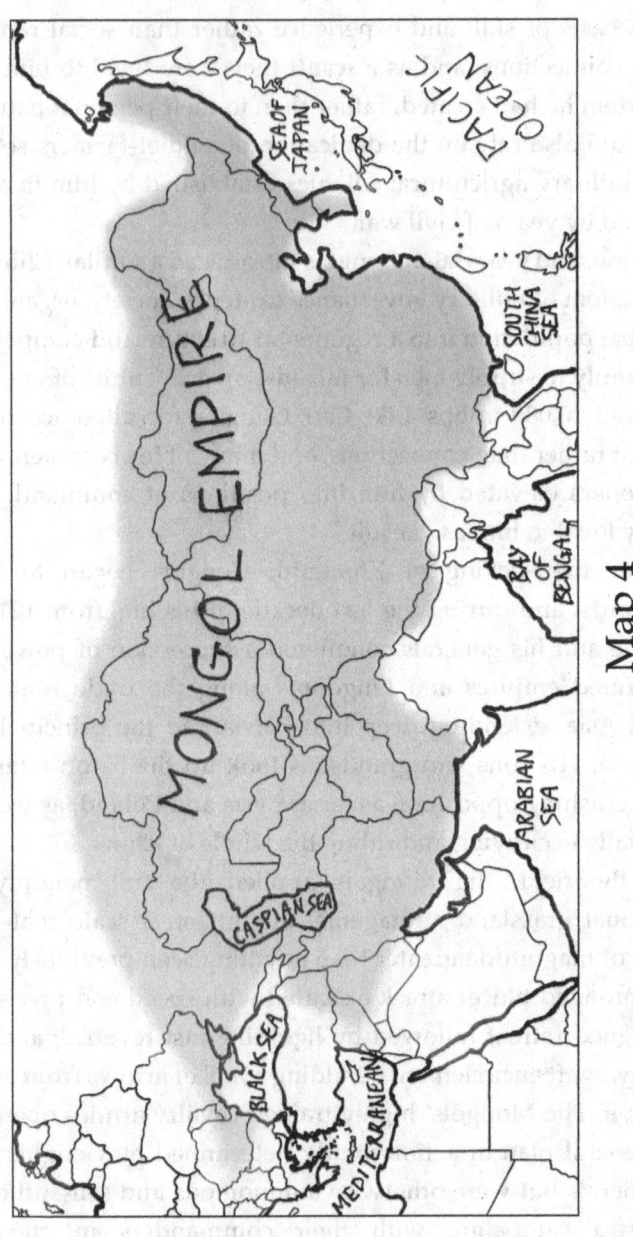

Map 4

The Mongol empire circa 1290

Genghis Khan's organized, methodical approach to waging war and ruling the lands he conquered, was probably the single most significant factor in his success. It enabled him to scale-up the traditional techniques of a steppe raiding party to meet the strategic and operational needs of an army of up to 100,000 mounted archers, and it allowed him to structure an empire that expanded and held fast for several generations after his death in 1227. From virtually nothing—there was no Mongol polity on the grasslands to begin with—he founded a state geared to military conquest, and forged a fighting force that had no match across the length and breadth of the landmass.

Genghis appears to have shaped his organizational approach through the course of his initially faltering campaigns against the sinicized Tanguts (1207-1209) and then the Jurchen rulers of Northern China (1211-1215). His strategic and organizational thinking during those years would have been deeply informed by what he learned of mass-population warfare and state administration from the Chinese officers and advisers he gathered during those campaigns. The teachings of Sun Tzu almost certainly played a part.

communication via relays of mounted couriers. This enabled them to execute complex, articulated maneuvers in a way that confounded opponents and ensured that when battle was finally joined, the advantage always lay with the Mongols, whether in numbers, surprise, terrain or other respect.

Faced with defenders behind city walls, the Mongols were increasingly able to deploy the world's most technically advanced siege machinery, built on-site by their travelling corps of Chinese, and later Muslim, siege engineers. Where possible, they simply terrorized cities into submission, herding panic-stricken refugees ahead of them as they advanced, and making sure the inhabitants understood that Mongol commanders were in earnest when they offered a simple choice: open your gates or be exterminated. Several of the world's wealthiest, most sophisticated cities were razed by the Mongols, and their populations massacred. But the preferred policy under Genghis, for those who submitted early, was to eliminate only the feudal and military elite and then grant vassal-like autonomy to those who remained, offering security in return for a commitment to provide future Mongol armies with troops and logistical support, along with a steady supply of tribute goods for their Mongol overlords.

That blend of grassland speed and mobility, combined with Chinese technology and organization, and magnified by Genghis's own brilliance as a soldier, strategist, and political leader, gave the Mongols a decisive advantage over every opponent they encountered west of China. Despite one or two setbacks, their military superiority during the period of expansion, as measured in technology, organization, leadership, strategy and capacity to adapt, was complete. As a result, the nature of war was transformed wherever they fought. In Europe, the arrival of Mongol-led forces, which outwitted and crushed the most powerful armies sent against them, put an end to the era of heavily armoured, mounted knights. And at the other end of the landmass, the Mongols' protracted war against the Song empire in southern China, spurred innovations in gunpowder technology which led both sides to deploy the world's first explosive artillery shells, in the form of gunpowder-packed iron casings catapulted from siege engines.

Antecedents for the Mongols' military success
Recognizing Sun Tzu-type strategy and tactics in the Mongols' pan-continental expansion, is one thing. Attributing the Mongols' military success to principles and approaches derived from the treatise, is another altogether, and on this we can only speculate. But it is entirely possible, and even likely, that Genghis Khan had access to, and made use of, the Chinese war manual.

Discipline and deception were already inherent in the Mongol way of fighting, honed through generations of grassland feuding and raids. Similarly, speed and mobility were a given among the mounted marauders of the steppes. But the skills of mass military organization, which in a few short years converted a cobbled-together horde of disputatious tribes into an all-conquering military machine, were surely learned, both directly and indirectly, from the Chinese—which almost certainly means that Sun Tzu played a part.

Genghis Khan knew, as well as any military commander in history, how to control and exploit the evolving strategic dynamic of a conflict—from accumulating physical and psychological advantages before battle, to ensuring that victory was inevitable once battle was joined.

His leadership qualities were clearly also a factor in the Mongols' military success, and he does in many ways approximate to the traits of the ideal Sun Tzu commander. We may never know for sure if Genghis Khan was inspired by what he learned of the Sun Tzu fighting philosophy from his Tangut and Chinese aides, but there are tantalizing glimpses of Sun Tzu-type metaphors and phrasing among his edicts and correspondence.

In one edict Genghis declared: "He who is able to command ten men in battle formation will be able to command a thousand or ten thousand in battle formation, and he deserves such a command" — which evokes Sun Tzu's: "Commanding a mass of troops on the battlefield is the same as commanding a small detachment" (ch. 5.1).

In a letter to a Taoist prelate in China whose moral guidance he was seeking, in 1219, Genghis wrote: "I care for the common people as I would for an infant, and I look after my men as if we were brothers", which echoes a similar sentiment in Sun Tzu: "When a commander is as mindful of the safety of his troops as if they were infants...when he values their lives as if they were his own sons..." (ch. 10.4).

On another occasion Genghis was recorded as telling his two most trusted generals: "You two are to me as the shafts of a cart," recalling Sun Tzu's metaphor for a good general as a "brace on the chariot of state" (ch. 3.4).

The first translation
There is also the curious fact that the very first translation of the *Sun-tzu* from Chinese into any other language, was the Tangut version, produced in woodblock-print format shortly before the Tanguts fell under Mongol dominion. This was also the period when the first woodblock editions of the Chinese text, printed during the Southern Song dynasty (1127-1279), were bringing the treatise to a greatly expanded Chinese readership.

We know that while Genghis was illiterate, he actively recruited the service of scribes and commissioned the development of the Mongol script as part of his nation-building programme. He made a point of personally interviewing captive scholars and experts and drawing them into the ranks of his advisers, among them his principal political counsellor, Yelü Chucai, a Khitan noble who had served northern China's Jurchen government as a scholar-official. The Khitans, who were culturally related to the Mongols, had themselves ruled a large swathe of northern China until supplanted by the Jurchen in 1125.

We know that Genghis avidly adopted innovations in the science of warfare, that he worked hard to understand his opponents, and that he prepared meticulously with his generals to counter enemy strategy and tactics. We can then presume that Genghis, in the years after subjugating the Tanguts and while challenging the Jurchen rulers of northern China, would have evinced an interest in the teachings of China's most prestigious military classic.

What is certain is that after the 1207-1209 campaign against the Tanguts, and within a few years of the Sun Tzu treatise first appearing in Tangut translation, the Mongols, under Genghis Khan's leadership, transformed themselves from a talented rabble into an unprecedentedly dominant military force and rewrote the history of the Euro-Asian continent.

Sun Tzu could well have been with them.

Napoleon

Nearly six centuries later, events in Europe uncannily echoed Genghis Khan's rise in Asia, soon after his likely exposure to the teachings of Sun Tzu. Within just a few years of the *Sun-tzu*'s first appearance in the West, in French translation, a military leader heralding a revolutionary new form of warfare emerged in France and rewrote the history of *his* continent.

The translation of Sun Tzu by the Jesuit Father J. J. M. Amiot was first published in Paris in 1772, under the title *Art Militaire des Chinois*, and it was republished there in 1782 in a compendium of Jesuit writings on China, two years before Napoleon Bonaparte arrived at the École Militaire in Paris as a cadet.

The translation had been well received, at a time when China was idealized in French liberal circles as a beacon of sophistication, and Napoleon, a studious young man with a voracious appetite for military history and theory, almost certainly would have come across it.

Napoleon never publicly referenced the treatise, and there is no evidence directly linking it to the evolution of his military thinking. Yet his style of command, and the innovations in organization and strategy that came to be associated with him, conform to an intriguing degree with the model outlined two millennia earlier by Sun Tzu, and could in many respects form a case-study of Sun Tzu's theories in action.

Military reform

When Napoleon graduated to his first commission in 1785, the French military had already been debating and experimenting with alternative structures of military governance and tactics for decades. In particular, the debacle for France of the Seven Years War (1756-1763) had cast doubt over the *Ancien Régime* convention of fixed, linear patterns of engagement between cumbersome armies, ponderously maneuvered into position.

French military planners believed they could unlock added destructive potential by allowing individual men and units greater scope to operate autonomously, in a coordinated fashion, so as to improve mobility and expedite the tactical concentration and dispersal of forces as required.

One early reform that proved especially effective was the introduction of light infantry, licensed to swarm in open order against the enemy's parade-ground ranks, pinning the enemy down with gunfire while their own commanders took measure of the situation and maneuvered for advantage.

The French Revolution, beginning in 1789, broke out in the middle of this process of reform and at a stroke cleared the way for the take-over of France's aristocratic military apparatus by a generation of ambitious, nationalistic, professionally-trained junior officers. They were ready to apply a new philosophy of war and soon became battle-hardened in the course of the Republic's desperate fight to survive through a succession of Revolutionary Wars (1792-1802).

During this period, France became the first country in Europe to institutionalize a new mode of national mobilization — the *levée en masse*, or general conscription.

Napoleon rode the crest of this wave of military reform and by the time he reached the pinnacle of command, in 1799, France was able to deploy the continent's largest mass of experienced military manpower, configured for rapid wars of aggression and led by motivated, innovative generals, several of whom turned out to be as brilliant, and as lucky, as Napoleon himself.

Organizational innovation
The new organizational structure found its fullest expression in

the *corps d'armée* system, introduced by Napoleon during his first year as head of state and commander-in-chief.

The corps were semi-autonomous, scaled-down armies featuring a full complement of armed contingents and support services. In a manner reminiscent of Genghis Khan's nomad cavalry, several corps would advance in loose, *bataillon carré* (battalion square) formation, with the individual corps often dozens of miles apart but always in close communication. They moved fast and travelled light, living off the land in the approved Sun Tzu manner rather than lingering to establish secure supply lines. ("An astute general provisions his forces at the enemy's expense" – ch. 2.3.) They could quickly alter their plans and were less prone to the logistical vulnerabilities of their cumbersome rivals.

Each corps was able to do battle independently, but the system's greatest strength lay in the tightly drilled discipline and skill with which the corps coordinated their maneuvers, converging rapidly into attack formation once the enemy had been definitively located.

Typically, the aim would be to outflank the opposing army and concentrate maximum force against one of its weaker points, severing lines of communication and supply and disrupting the enemy's equilibrium before its commanders had time to properly assess and respond to the threat.

The articulated *corps d'armée* system was ideally suited to the flexible patterns of maneuver of France's revolutionary armies, in contrast to the stiff formations and lumbering movements of Europe's classic, *Ancien Régime* armies, and it enabled Napoleon to ensure his soldiers already had the upper hand even before battle was joined. In Sun Tzu terms, his armies almost always arrived at the battlefield with the strategic momentum on their side. ("A winning force first secures victory, then goes into battle" – ch. 4.2.)

Tactical and strategic genius

In 1805, Napoleon — who had by now crowned himself Emperor — marched the seven corps of his *Grande Armée*, originally collected near the Channel for an invasion of England, eastwards into the domains of the three continental powers: Austria, Russia and Prussia. In his first major test of the campaign he captured an Austrian army, intact, at the southern German city of Ulm in just three days in October of that year, having first bewildered his opponents with lightning-fast advances on several fronts, before swiftly converging and then enveloping them.

Within a month the *Grande Armée* was in Vienna, and in early December fought and won a decisive battle against the Russian and Austrian allied forces at Austerlitz, in what is now the Czech Republic.

Napoleon's success at Austerlitz, the pivotal victory of his career, hinged on the psychological gambit by which he brought the numerically superior Allies to battle on his timetable and at a location of his choosing. Concealing the fact that he was in more of a hurry to do battle than his opponents, who had the benefit of comprehensive logistical support and were anticipating strong reinforcements, Napoleon feigned weakness and hesitation, putting out feelers for peace negotiations in a way reminiscent of Cao Cao before the battle of Huayin in AD 211.

Emboldened by their opponent's apparent vulnerability, the Allies attacked, committing a sizeable share of their forces to what turned out to be a strategic sideshow on the French right flank, while exposing themselves to attack on the Pratzen Heights, a crucial area of high ground in the centre. The French held out long enough on the right for Napoleon to deploy a mass of hitherto concealed battalions and to successfully storm the Heights, as planned, and from there he successively divided, confused and defeated the Austrian and Russian forces to his left

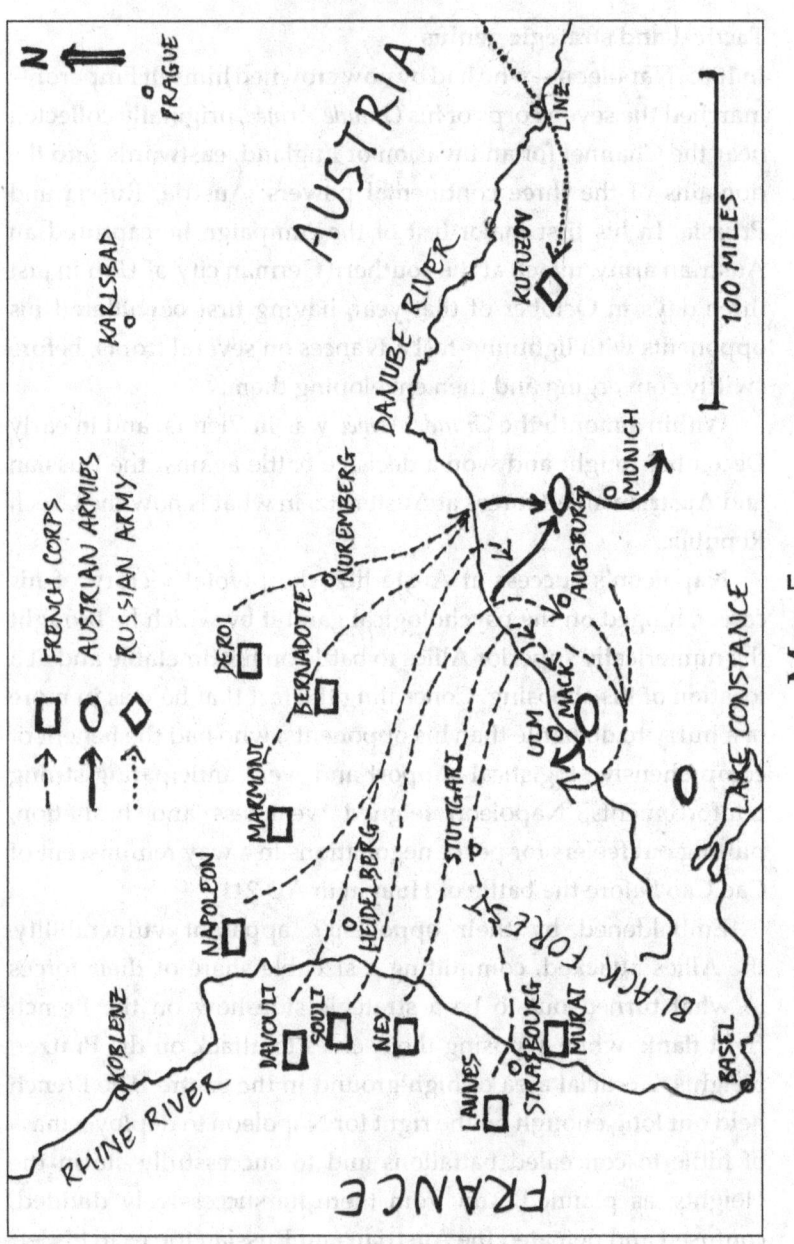

Map 5

Napoleon at Ulm, 1805

"The military ideal is to force an opposing army to submit without battle." (ch. 3.1)

The pivotal battle of Napoleon's career was his victory over the emperors of Russia and Austria at Austerlitz, in early December 1805. But it was his non-battle at Ulm in southern Germany, around six weeks earlier, that was arguably the greater strategic achievement.

Napoleon's army of 210,000 men, divided into seven corps and spread across a 100-mile front, had raced from its base in Boulogne, aiming to confront the Austrians before they could link up with their Russian allies. The lead commander on the Austrian side, General Mack, with Ulm as the centrepiece of his defensive preparations, anticipated blocking the French after they crossed the upper Rhine and advanced eastwards through the Black Forest. But events moved faster than Mack, or any of the traditional European armies, could comprehend. Napoleon crossed the river north of the Black Forest, swept past Ulm, then wheeled south and west as his corps converged, cutting Mack off from Russian support and trapping him in the city. With no major battle, the Austrian army was captured intact.

The tightly coordinated operational autonomy of Napoleon's fast-moving corps, allowing them to fan out and close in at will, delivered as much of a shock to the conventional way of warfare in Europe as the lightning-fast maneuvers of Genghis and his generals had in Central Asia and China, centuries earlier.

and right.

The day was not without blunders and missed opportunities on both sides, but at every crunch point the French showed sufficient resolve, mobility and coordination to seize the tactical initiative, just as their commander-in-chief expected them to.

Inviting the attack on his right flank early in the day was a calculated gamble, and it paid off handsomely. At the age of thirty-six, Napoleon had humbled the combined might of the Austrian and Russian empires and now controlled most of south and central Europe. His method, as much as anyone could grasp it, appeared to be a devilishly effective combination of organizational efficiency, tactical guile and strategic preparation, all compounded and enhanced by the sheer confidence and aggressiveness of the French armies and of Napoleon himself.

An aura of genius and invincibility now attached to Napoleon, and it was consolidated the following year, 1806, when the French demolished the armies of Prussia—France's sole unbeaten rival on the continent—at the twin battles of Jena and Auerstädt and during the ensuing advance on the Prussian capital.

After days of probing maneuvers, with the French pressing but neither side certain of the other's whereabouts, the French main force located and engaged a Prussian flanking contingent (which Napoleon mistook to be the Prussian main force) at Jena, while the Prussian main force under King Frederick William ran into General Davout's isolated French corps (which the Prussians assumed was the French main force) on the road 15 miles away at Auerstädt. The French, adaptable by habit and drilled for flexibility, fared better in these unscripted circumstances than their slow-reacting Prussian counterparts, whose battalions were still geared for the stately maneuvers and predictable dispositions of the Seven-Years-War era.

Napoleon, as ever, controlled the tempo of the conflict, using

CHRISTOPHER MACDONALD

his advantage in speed and mobility to keep the Prussians on the back foot, while seeking to force them into battle sooner rather than later. But the battle at Jena was no foregone conclusion. Half way through the fighting, after a morning of attacks and counterattacks from both sides, the Prussian general Hohenlohe passed up an opportunity to advance in strength against a stretched French line, preferring to await reinforcements. In the event, it was the French who received reinforcements first and regained the initiative, and by 3pm that day Hohenlohe's battalions were in retreat, half of his men having been killed, wounded or captured.

At Auerstädt, meanwhile, the Prussian king, Frederick William, also erred disastrously on the side of caution. A point came in the battle when he had an opportunity to overwhelm the French by counterattacking with the infantry battalions and artillery batteries he had in reserve, but he declined to do so, mistakenly believing that he was facing Napoleon in person. The heavily outnumbered French under Davout then launched a fresh wave of attacks along the length of their line, eventually taking the high ground and causing the Prussians to withdraw in disorder.

The French went on to crush the bulk of the fleeing Prussian army and occupy Berlin, and over the following months Napoleon advanced eastwards through Poland, wiping out most of the Russian army and imposing a peace deal on the Tsar, in 1807, that recognized French control as far as the Russian border. This was the high-water mark of Napoleon's military success.

That same year, however, saw the start of France's resource-sapping involvement in Spain, in which French military strength proved unequal to a determined insurgency waged by guerrilla ("little war") fighters backed by the British. The shifting coalitions of continental powers, scenting weakness, began to reassert themselves. In 1809, Napoleon had to turn his focus

75

away from Spain to suppress a challenge from the resurgent Austrian empire, and then again in 1812 when he led the *Grande Armée*, bolstered to over half a million men, on an ill-conceived invasion of Russia.

Returning to France after the humiliating retreat from Moscow, having sacrificed all but a fraction of his vast army (as well as having lost Spain in the army's absence), Napoleon launched a new round of conscription and went on the attack again, aiming to reinvigorate his imperial project. This time, however, his enemies all rounded on him at once, eventually cornering him in Paris in 1814 and forcing him to abdicate.

He briefly reappeared the following year, inspiring a reunion of his corps for a final flourish of tactical flair and aggression at Waterloo, but this time his luck had run out. Napoleon gambled on a quick offensive to separate the Anglo-allied and Prussian armies, under Wellington and Blücher respectively, then defeat one after the other.

It was a maneuver of the kind that had been successful for him many times before, but on this occasion the gamble did not pay off. Wellington's men held firm under sustained pressure throughout the long day, and Prussian reinforcements arrived in time to break the momentum of the French with a flank attack, turning the tide decisively in favour of the Allies.

Sun Tzu hallmarks

Napoleon's approach to warfare bore many of the hallmarks of the Sun Tzu ideal. Like Genghis Khan and Cao Cao before him, he developed a reputation for military genius on the back of speed and mobility of his armies, on his record of more battles won than lost, and on his tactical flair and strategic brilliance. Morale was strong wherever he was in command, and after his early successes the mystique that preceded him into battle often scrambled his opponents' sense of judgement, giving the French a psychological advantage before the first shots were fired.

For Napoleon, as for those earlier renowned commanders, victory was the single, total, non-negotiable objective, to the exclusion of all other concerns. He had no scruples about, for example, tricking the Austrian and Russian emperors at Austerlitz into thinking he was ready to sue for peace, or about encouraging his marksmen at Jena to deliberately pick off officers in the Prussian line, which the Prussians considered unsporting.

He prepared scrupulously before every battle, absorbing intelligence reports, analysing his opponents' strengths and weaknesses and closely studying the terrain, yet he combined extremely cautious preparations with dazzling audacity in the field. Time and again he shaped the strategic dynamic of the battle to his own advantage, seizing the initiative and imposing his will on the enemy.

He varied his tactics and formations, mixing frontal with oblique attacks, rapidly dispersing and concentrating his contingents, flexibly adapting his formations, so as to continually surprise and confuse his opponents, making it impossible for them to ever confidently predict his next move.

He baited enemies into impulsive errors and wrong-footed them with feints, before rounding on them with an unexpectedly swift flanking maneuver, or — just when they were expecting such a maneuver and hastening to reinforce their flanks — pouring his troops in through the centre.

And he fluidly orchestrated the movements of tens of thousands of men at a time, leading them, in the words of Sun Tzu, "as if guiding a single person by the hand" (ch. 11.4).

But Napoleon's record of aggressive success also concealed weaknesses of the kind warned against by Sun Tzu, that were to be his undoing.

For example, the destructive campaigns back and forth across continental Europe, though largely victorious, multiplied his enemies, inspired them to copy his tactics, and incited them to unite and eventually avenge themselves on France.

He relied for his wars of expansion on repeated rounds of compulsory conscription to replenish his battered armies, but this policy became less and less tenable as one war followed another.

He was obsessed with trying to humble Great Britain, but his efforts to blockade the old enemy by sealing the entire continent against British commerce, backfired, leading indirectly to his unwinnable campaign in Spain and the catastrophic invasion of Russia.

And it can only have been hubris that caused him to believe he could bring the Russians to heel by pursuing them to Moscow, in the face of the approaching Russian winter.

Up until at least 1807, Napoleon probably came as close as any general in history to matching the Sun Tzu archetype. But battlefield brilliance is not enough, and events during the latter part of Napoleon's career demonstrated that he was not a commander who, in the manner of Sun Tzu, appreciated the virtue of "forc[ing] an opposing army to submit without battle" (ch. 3.1). On the contrary, he seemed conditioned above all to fight, and to continue fighting until he lost. For that reason he was destined to lead his country to eventual defeat.

As Sun Tzu reminded readers two millennia before Napoleon, the best generals are often not those most widely celebrated in their own day. Indeed, their victories "earn them neither a reputation for wisdom nor accolades for courage", for they always seem, because of careful planning, to face "foes who are already beaten" (ch. 4.2).

Aspects of the Sun Tzu doctrine can be discerned anywhere in history that large, well-organized armies have been commanded by bold, innovative generals specializing in unbalancing strong opponents by means of strategic positioning, mental cunning and sharp maneuvers. The militarists of East Asia, in classical times, were certainly conversant with the Sun Tzu approach to war and willing to put it into practice, and in the campaigns of both Genghis Khan and Napoleon we see key tenets of the treatise in action — whether or not due to its direct influence.

But a counter-doctrine — the attritional, blunt-force approach to armed conflict associated with Western military thinkers like Carl von Clausewitz — was also to be found in ancient East Asia, and it too influenced the creation of the Mongol empire and the events of the Napoleonic Wars.

The military machine will always, by its own internal logic, tend towards blunt force as the ultimate guarantor of success, rather than trusting fully to the mind-and-maneuvers approach. No commander wishes the enemy to enjoy numerical superiority, or more and better weaponry, and as even Sun Tzu notes: "An armed force strong enough to defy minor opponents, nevertheless falls prey to a major opponent." (ch. 3.3).

Thus it was that Napoleon's techniques for rapid, mass maneuver, despite initially liberating European armies from the ossified conventions of *Ancien Régime* warfare, ironically paved the way — via Clausewitz, industrialization and the advent of total war — for the blunt-force stalemate of World War I.

A similar sequence of events had unfolded in China between the sixth and third centuries BC, when warfare had transitioned from the traditional paradigm of the codified, chivalric duel, towards the complex strategic engagements of the Warring States era, and finally onto the primeval trials of strength, among colossal military entities, that culminated with the fusion of those states into an empire in 221 BC. It is a pattern which seems to have been repeated throughout military history. The tactical and strategic lessons of Sun Tzu are learned, then superseded by advances in military technology, and economic strength, and growing weight of men at arms, then learned again, and so on.

A case can be made to suggest that aspects of the Sun Tzu approach were rediscovered by the Japanese and German militarists of the 1930s, in reaction to the attritional quagmire of World War I, in the form of tactics designed to exploit the temporary advantage in speed and mobility made possible by modern, mechanized warfare. The British military historian and theorist Basil Liddell Hart first read Sun Tzu in 1927, and by some accounts it was his writings during the following decade that inspired the tactics behind Germany's *blitzkrieg* campaigns in the first year of World War II.

The North Vietnamese in the 1960s and 1970s, along with anti-colonial liberation forces around the world throughout the second half of the twentieth century, practiced permutations of the long-game mind-and-maneuvers approach to wear down and defeat impatient, powerful enemies, who tended to be over-equipped and under-motivated by comparison.

The strategic and tactical bible for many of those campaigns was Mao Zedong's essay, *On Guerrilla Warfare*, which, while not directly citing the *Sun-tzu*, channelled its key tenets: avoid decisive engagements with the enemy, ignore well-defended cities, have no perceptible dispositions, turn numerical inferiority to advantage by the asymmetrical application of force, unsettle the enemy with an incessant campaign of harassment and pressure, and refuse battle unless certain of winning.

That strategic lineage, from Sun Tzu by way of Mao, lives on in the combination of bandit guile and organizational sophistication, often complemented with millenarian fervour, that characterizes the campaigns of insurgency groups in the twenty-first century.

The armies of the world's present-day military powers have also absorbed concepts from Sun Tzu into their doctrines, as well as into the curricula of their military academies. This is true to some degree of the US army, but is even more true of China's PLA (People's Liberation Army), all of whose officers reportedly learn to recite Sun Tzu by heart.

Despite the periodic appearance throughout history of gifted generals practising strategic positioning combined with mind-and-maneuvers warfare, it appears that the world has never yet seen an unbeaten exponent of the Sun Tzu approach to war. Cao, Genghis and Napoleon came close, but each had his share of defects and defeats, and their victories were often costly — too much so for the innumerable victims of their abilities.

Perhaps those claims for invincible armies and the promise of conflicts won without battle, were hyperbole on the part of the author or authors behind the *Sun-tzu*. Or could it be, in Cao Cao's words, that the main thrust of the work still eludes us?

4
Sun Tzu and the PRC

War has moved on since the campaigns of Cao Cao, Genghis Khan and Napoleon. Industrial warfare, nuclear weapons, cyber war and the militarization of space have opened up new domains of conflict beyond the reckoning of Sun Tzu. Advances in artificial intelligence and robotics are redefining the human role in battle in ways which we cannot yet fully comprehend. And national armed forces are more likely these days to find themselves fighting irregular combatants dispersed among a civilian population, rather than confronting the massed men and machinery of an enemy state. The age of "modern" warfare may well be at an end.

Yet the age-old tactics of speed and surprise, bluffs and feints, and ambushes and asymmetry remain fundamental. Commanders with strategic and organizational nous are just as valued as they were two millennia ago. And Sun Tzu is today more widely read and discussed than ever.

This is particularly so in the PRC where there is a resurgence of interest in political and military ideas from the classical era, and where principles first articulated by Sun Tzu still influence national geopolitical strategy.

Strategic principles
The Sun Tzu treatise originated as both a campaign manual and a collection of strategy-related theories and discussions, in an age when strategy had yet to emerge as a distinct discipline. On the one hand it provided military professionals, and the princes or kings who retained them, with an inventory of well-known tactics and techniques for use on campaign, systematically

collated for study and reference. On the other hand, it was a quasi-philosophical guide to the underlying principles of warfare.

Familiarity with these principles allowed commanders to combine and innovate tactics indefinitely according to circumstance.

By emphasizing the meta-tactics of campaign-management, over and above operational tactics, the Sun Tzu treatise invited its students to broaden their perspective on war, seeing a campaign in terms of an extended contest of wit and will, one ultimately settled on the basis on decisions taken well in advance of any actual clash of arms.

Rather than focussing on the physical fact of the army, as a mass of men and armaments, the text instead asked military practitioners to consider a multitude of psychological, political and organizational variables influencing a state's capacity for battle, from the mental state of the men and commanders on both sides, to intelligence gathering, training and discipline, and the relationship between the state's military and sovereign authorities.

The *Sun-tzu* wasn't alone in addressing the influence of these variables on the outcome of a battle or campaign, but it did so more succinctly and systematically than other military texts of the period, and raised military planning to a new level of sophistication. Battle could now be analysed as one event, not necessarily decisive in itself, within a larger scheme of action. War, for the first time, became a primarily strategic challenge.

This was the understanding of strategy that shaped the paradigm of war during the Warring States period: an overarching and evolving scheme of action, beginning long before battle, aimed at accumulating advantage over the enemy.

Among the insights that emerged from this understanding of military strategy as a managed, long-term process, was a recognition of the importance of controlling both risk and cost.

Since the level of risk spikes during combat, when it is particularly difficult to anticipate and react to survival-threatening variables, the ideal is to secure such a big advantage over the enemy that battle itself becomes redundant: "The military ideal is to force an opposing army to submit without battle." (ch. 3.1).

And when battle is nevertheless necessary, the risk should be mitigated by limiting the scale and objective of the encounter, so as to prevent it from escalating to a decisive clash — the most risky kind of conflict.

As Sun Tzu emphasized, military struggle imposes costs on all involved, the extent of which can be difficult to anticipate and the consequences of which can be difficult to contain. The mutual costs of battle are particularly high between evenly-matched opponents. Combatants of this kind would be wise, therefore, to conserve energy and resources until they can be confident, through disciplined assessment, that they have an overwhelming advantage and that the eventual cost of the fight will be justified by the anticipated gains.

Planning to control long-term risks and costs in this way required re-imagining the sphere of battle to encompass non-military aspects of the contest, far in advance of any actual clash of arms, with the result that the secretive preparations and devious ploys of the military campaign began to spill into interstate politics and diplomacy. The consequences of this development were later catalogued in *The Stratagems of the Warring States*, a classic of statecraft which documented the political and diplomatic machinations of the period. Trust eroded among the polities of the Zhou realm, norms and institutions governing interstate cooperation withered, and the region sank into a spiral of warfare in which millions of lives were sacrificed.

Military strategy in the Warring States paradigm is therefore a process in which the urge to act against an adversary who threatens the survival of one's own state must be tempered by the need to first accumulate sufficient pre-battle advantage over that adversary, as well as the need to minimize the existential risks and costs that kinetic warfare poses to one's own side.

It is worth mentioning at this point that despite advocating the avoidance of battle in certain circumstances, the *Sun-tzu* is in no way a pacifist manifesto — it contains no reference to or interest in the concept of "peacetime", which in the Warring State paradigm can only be understood as a period of recovery from and preparation for war. That famous adjuration to force opponents into submission without fighting (sometimes misleadingly quoted as "winning without battle") was purely expedient.

The campaign-level insights of Sun Tzu can be summarized in two key principles, which form the cornerstone of China's traditional strategic culture and the basis of Chinese strategy to this day:

- Maximize your prospects of victory in war by stealthily accruing strategic advantage across the full political and military spectrum, well in advance of battle
- Minimize the risk and cost of war by aiming to achieve your aims without battle, where battle can be avoided, or by restricting your armies to limited objectives, where battle cannot be avoided.

These are complemented by three auxiliary principles, describing the characteristic Sun Tzu approach:

- Be prudent and pragmatic in your preparations for war

- Be flexible and unpredictable in strategy and tactics
- Be willing to sacrifice small advantages now, for big gains later.

These principles guide campaign planning, in terms of processes and approaches, but do not dictate specific policies and actions. As Sun Tzu emphasizes, every conflict is unique and demands a different combination of tactics. The overall approach — victory through strategic dominance — is consistent, but that approach involves "more variations that could ever be known" (ch. 5.2).

Strategic narrative
Classical teachings are back in favour in China, after an interval of decades, but the Warring States paradigm of interstate relations, and the strategic principles traditionally attached to it, never really went away. Both underpin the narrative by which the Chinese Communist Party (CCP) today asserts control over the country and rationalizes its contemporary geopolitical ambitions.

That narrative tells how China, having been rescued by the CCP from the grip of powerful enemies in the 20th century, has recovered its internal strength and is now in the process of prevailing over those enemies, one by one, and ensuring that they will never threaten China again. It views the world through a Sun Tzu-tinted, Warring States lens, in which the 21st-century *tianxia*, or "world-under-heaven", remains a fundamentally hostile realm of competing polities, each maximizing their own national interest and all scrabbling to dominate. Alliances, in this modern narrative just as in the ancient Sun Tzu, are purely expedient, and the only assurance of national security comes from relative power, measured both in economic and military strength.

Since there cannot be two hegemons in such a world, the United States — the most formidable of China's competitors in this modern narrative — will ultimately have to make way for its resurgent rival. The United States, according to the narrative, realizes the danger that it faces and is therefore pitting its economic, political and military might against China, aiming to contain its rising power and retard China's return to global pre-eminence. China meanwhile, still temporarily the weaker party, counters with its own campaign of economic, political and military gambits, aiming to outwit and outflank its adversary.

The physical front line of the confrontation described in this narrative lies along China's maritime periphery, which arcs from Japan and Korea to the South China Sea, with the strategically decisive island of Taiwan in the center of the field of play. That arc of islands and sea, which is where the two sides increasingly bump up against each other and where the potential for open hostilities is greatest, is therefore the focus of China's geopolitical strategy.

Unsurprisingly, the PRC does not publish a clear strategic plan for dislodging the United States from the maritime periphery en route to realizing its wider geopolitical ambitions. Yet the various strands of China's overarching strategic narrative provide circumstantial evidence for the existence of just such a Grand Scheme.

There is the official, glorified narrative of "national rejuvenation" — now branded the China Dream — in which China is fully restored to global pre-eminence in time for the hundredth anniversary, in 2049, of the CCP's civil war victory and founding of the People's Republic of China. There is the accompanying nationalist narrative, transmitted through the nationwide Patriotic Education campaign, which has been shaping the attitudes of Chinese youth towards the US and Japan, in particular, since the 1990s. And there is the revanchist narrative of reclaimed sovereignty and territorial integrity, driving the ambitions of China's armed forces as they incrementally advance the perimeters of PRC control across the East and South China Seas, in the face of poorly coordinated opposition from the United States and its regional allies.

In each case, there are tell-tale signs of the strategic approach articulated in the *Sun-tzu*: maximize your long-term advantages, minimize risk and cost, and proceed in ways that are as prudent and pragmatic as they are unpredictable and flexible.

The China Dream
The China Dream of national rejuvenation, frequently invoked by the current team of CCP leaders, is a vision of a future China which not only provides all its people with a decent standard of living, including standards of education, healthcare, social support, environmental protections and other services expected in any developed nation, but also a China which dominates East Asia and tops the global tables for wealth and influence. In effect, the Dream promises to re-set the hierarchy of international power back to the early 19th century, before Western aggression pitched China into its "Hundred Years of National Humiliation".

The Dream promises implicitly that today's Western-oriented international norms and the institutions that embody them such as the United Nations and World Bank, will by 2049 have been modified or replaced to reflect a more "multipolar" (i.e. more China-centric) world order. Mandarin will be well on its way to supplanting English as the global language of commerce, the renminbi will have taken over from the US dollar as the international reserve currency of choice, Taiwan will be governed from Beijing, and the CCP will of course still be in charge.

The narrative depicts a future world overseen, but not bullied, by a virtuous and non-hegemonic China. Part of the appeal of this account is that it appears to be supported by present trends. China is already on a par with the United States in economic terms, when compared at purchasing power parity (PPP) exchange rates, and if present rates of growth continue then China's US-dollar GDP will overtake that of the United States at some point during the 2020s (although on a per capita basis it will still be poorer). The PLA, meanwhile, has rapidly transformed from the low-tech, infantry-heavy military of the early 1990s, into today's high-tech, networked force bristling with air, naval, cyber and counter-space capabilities, with a budget that has quadrupled in the past 15 years. Growth trajectories do therefore suggest that China could outrank the US as an economic power by 2049, and could conceivably have surpassed it militarily, just as the China Dream promises.

But there is also a parallel, darker version of the Dream, in which China only realizes its goals in the teeth of bitter opposition from the status quo powers left over from the 20th century. Those powers, the darker version declares, are already using every device at their disposal to stymie China's "peaceful rise," including: military harassment to pin the PRC back against its coastline and prevent it from acquiring the ocean access and maritime territories that are its birth-right; politically motivated protectionism to deny Chinese firms a fair opportunity in overseas markets and slow China's economic growth; anti-China alliances designed to encircle or contain China and restrict China's access to essential resources; false accusations about PRC-government-directed cyber-attacks and military-industrial espionage against targets in the West; and funds and support for "separatist forces" in Taiwan, Hong Kong, Tibet and Xinjiang, as well as for "anti-Chinese" civil rights advocates, in order to undermine CCP authority and push China into chaos.

The US in particular, fearing China's resurgence and anxious to preserve its ill-gotten hegemony over the globe, will, according to this narrative, ramp up its levels of threat and aggression towards China, leading to a war which China — better-prepared and with "moral and political authority" (ch. 1.2) on its side — will win.

This politically realist, Warring States vision of the future excites far more attention within China than the official, rose-tinted version of the Dream. Perhaps more disturbing is the fact that it is continually fuelled via the CCP-controlled domains of the media and academia, as well as within the PLA, and among tens of millions of febrile, nationalist netizens in the echo chamber of the country's tightly monitored and heavily censored domestic Internet.

It is a vision that packs emotional appeal powered by a myth of national victimhood along with unapologetic chauvinism (both stoked by PRC authorities), and it implicitly promises that the ghosts of the "Hundred Years of National Humiliation" will not simply be laid to rest by China's restoration, but will be avenged. The Taiwan separatists will be crushed, the Japanese dwarf pirates will pay for their atrocities, and the insufferably arrogant Americans will have to learn their place in a new world order. Meanwhile China's earlier colonial-era tormentors, such as the British and French, will simply be obliged to acknowledge their pitiful smallness and condemned to an eternity of petty humiliations, in a process which is already well under way.

Given that the relevant channels for public discourse within China come under the direct control or supervision of the party-state authorities, it is fair to assume that this narrative of the future, firmly rooted in China's Warring States past, has the Party's blessing. It is a narrative which conjures up Sun Tzu's single-minded focus on out-competing opponents, in an arena of ruthless conflict where all are trying to dominate, and at the same time accords with the vision of the world that China's ruling party needs its public to share.

That darker version of the Dream conforms with the impression of a nation relishing its newly bulked-up geopolitical physique and keen to flex its muscles. The PRC used to be known for taking a low profile approach to international affairs, in line with Deng Xiaoping's dictum (framed in deliberate, Warring States phrasing) that China would be wise to "shroud its brightness and cultivate obscurity" (*tao guang yang hui*, 韜光養晦). That was at the beginning of the 1990s, during an earlier phase of modernization, when China's economy was much smaller than it is today and its armed forces were far less formidable. Nowadays, by contrast, PRC diplomatic and military representatives often opt for swagger over discretion, particularly for matters close to home. The foreign ministry regularly berates "small countries" in the region for having the temerity to challenge "big country" China's position on the South China Sea, while senior PLA officers appear to have free rein to wax belligerent about the "sea of fire" and other treats that await China's "enemies" — meaning the United States and Japan — should they interpose themselves into China's affairs in the South China Sea or the Taiwan Strait. That message is backed up with increasingly proactive measures to assert control over disputed maritime zones, from constructing airstrips and artificial islands to pushing the envelope for air and naval maneuvers, all depicted within the confines of the PRC news bubble as defensive responses to the hegemonic provocations of China's adversaries.

Regardless of the sunny rhetoric of the China Dream narrative, therefore, the PRC's rulers seem to prefer the general public to conceive of national rejuvenation, at least partially, in terms of a zero-sum struggle between China and the US-led Western world. A struggle for which their country can legitimately deploy the full Sun Tzu toolkit of strategy and tactics, both military and non-military. Not so much a Cold War, as a patient, steadily intensifying pre-war of mind and manipulation against a powerful but unfocused foe—who appears only dimly aware that the contest is under way.

Patriotic Education

The Tiananmen "Incident" of 1989 exposed the CCP's Achilles' heel—its shaky legitimacy in an age of mobility and accountability, when people are increasingly unwilling to simply accept the argument of "the mandate of heaven" as sufficient qualification for governing the state. The CCP regime has never been voted for and can't be voted out, so when students in Beijing demonstrated against corruption and economic inequity that year, their protests attracted popular support and were taken up in cities throughout China.

At about that same time, another large communist party was imploding just across the border in the soon-to-be-former USSR. After weeks of equivocation, hardliners among the CCP leadership prevailed over reformers, framed the crisis as a matter of survival or extinction for their party-state, and mobilized the PLA to crush the protests. The crackdown was then pushed down the national memory hole, to join the official non-recollection of other post-1949, CCP-inflicted miseries.

To ensure it stayed there, Party strategists devised a campaign of "patriotic education," initially focussing on the school curriculum and later broadened into a society-wide mobilization of media, cultural and social platforms—film and TV, exhibitions, publications, museums, commemorative events, propaganda drives and more. The idea was to redirect resentment away from domestic authorities and instead towards the foreign forces who had plagued the Manchu empire and Republican China during the colonial era, and who in the present day were still theoretically plotting to prevent Chinese people from ever recovering their rightful prosperity, power and international prestige.

Japan, whose brutal occupation of China before and during World War II remained a living memory, was — and is — a particular focus of the campaign. An ideology of "national humiliation" was cultivated, requiring every citizen, the young in particular, to internalize a fresh sense of grievance against those foreign powers, and to buy into the notion that China had unfinished business to settle with them. The theme of a great, noble empire enfeebled by devious, plundering barbarians before eventually bouncing back, was in any case a mainstay of China's national historical consciousness, so the new ideology took root on fertile ground. A narrative of nationalism retroactively replaced class struggle as Communist China's founding faith and became the Party's core legitimizing rationale.

Asserting the righteousness of one's own military and political leaders during wartime, in contrast to the devious and demonic ways of the enemy, would have been age-old doctrine even in Sun Wu's day. This is why the first chapter of the *Sun-tzu* identifies moral and political authority (which "rallies people behind their leader and motivates them to stake their lives for him" - ch. 1.2) as the very first factor by which to assess a state's prospects in a coming war. Extending that approach across years or even decades of patriotic education, however, as part of the strategic long game against an unwary adversary, was an innovation honed during the centuries of war among the Zhou states.

The archetype of this approach was the sovereign of the fifth-century-BC state of Yue, Goujian (勾踐), who, in a story known to every Chinese schoolchild, patiently nourished his hatred for the rival state of Wu, which had subjugated his homeland and humiliated him personally. For years, Goujian slept on a mat of twigs and licked dried gallbladder in the morning to daily renew his bitterness, and this continued long after the two states had made peace. Prudently and pragmatically, Goujian rebuilt trust with the king of Wu while stealthily adding to Yue's wealth and strength. When the opportunity came, he launched a strategically and tactically astute offensive against Wu, sacked its capital and permanently wiped Wu from the map.

Themes of patriotism and revenge are as interwoven in the story of Goujian as they are in the CCP's account of its own right to rule. It is a story in which the Party rises from humble beginnings to become the saviour of the Chinese nation, defeating an evil invader (Japan) and deposing a cruel tyrant (Chiang Kai-shek), before reviving the nation militarily and economically. A return of Japanese ultra-nationalism or of organized political opposition to the CCP, if either were to happen, would actually help the CCP by reinvigorating its case for ruling China in the 21st century. Until then, the US remains the mother lode of alleged "external forces" undermining CCP authority and threatening PRC survival – the chief antagonist that the master narrative of nationalism demands.

Most international analysts, and not a few Chinese, tend to believe that the United States has played a constructive role in China's extraordinary enrichment since the 1970s. The US has also been supportive in various ways towards the aspirations of ordinary Chinese for the kinds of social and political freedoms that are the norm in most of the developed world. But officially, within China, the US is viewed with suspicion and resentment, as a "hegemon" keeping the country militarily encircled and geopolitically constrained. Patriotic education helps the party-state to cement in people's minds the image of the US as an anti-China aggressor. And even though the party and business elite are happy to expatriate some of their wealth to the US, parachute their offspring into US higher education, and favour the US as an emigration destination of choice for themselves and their extended families, they continually invoke the US as a real and present threat to China's core interests, actively summoning up that ancient paradigm of zero-sum interstate competition in an anarchic "world-under-heaven".

Two decades of patriotic education have seeded China's youth, at least superficially, with a virulent strain of state-mandated nationalism, compatible with a powerful sense of exceptionalism that long pre-dates the CCP. China's businesses and institutions, not to mention tens of millions of well-educated young people, all get the underlying message. Should they choose to believe and behave as if their country is in a state of undeclared war with the US, and adopt stealthy, Sun Tzu-type strategic measures in response, they have the implicit endorsement of the party-state for doing so.

Reclaiming the maritime periphery

A third strand of the strategic narrative for overcoming China's principal rival is the mostly military project of restricting and eventually preventing the US Navy and Air Force from freely operating along China's maritime periphery, beginning with the area within the first island chain. The chain runs south from the main islands of Japan, down the line of the Ryukyus to Taiwan, crosses the Bashi channel then tracks the western coast of the Philippine archipelago as far as Malaysian Borneo. It embraces what the PRC considers to be home waters – the Yellow Sea, East China Sea and South China Sea. For PRC strategists, national

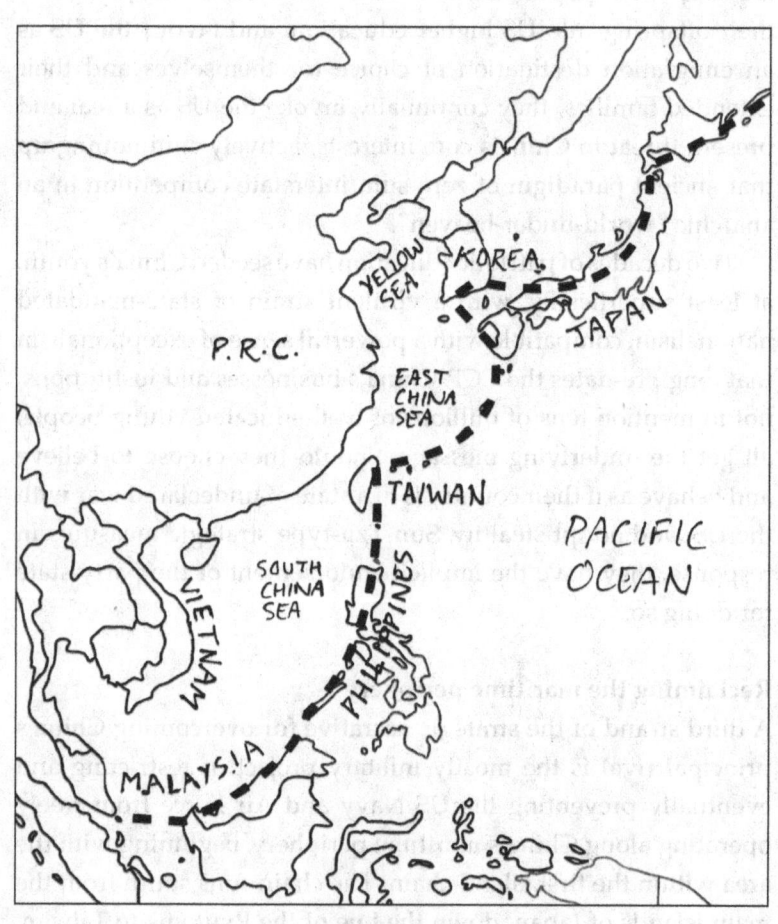

Map 6

China and the first island chain

The Pax Americana imposed by US military and economic alliances along the first island chain has helped to dampen down military competition within the region, prevent nuclear proliferation, and provide the stability necessary for the region's vaulting economic development. Such has been the status quo for several decades, and the PRC has arguably been its greatest beneficiary. It was political stability and open sea lanes along China's maritime periphery, along with the region's burgeoning prosperity, that enabled the country to pick itself up from the wreckage of the Mao years and successfully re-engage with the world through its coastal provinces.

From the perspective of PLA planners, however, the status quo has served its purpose and needs changing. That necklace of US military and political alliances is a choke chain keeping China within the confines of its coastal waters. National security requires that China never again risks being dominated from its maritime approaches, as it was by colonial powers until the mid-twentieth century, and this means that the PRC must ultimately take control of the passages through which its military forces and merchant shipping access the Pacific and Indian Oceans. In other words, from a PRC viewpoint, the US needs to be dislodged from its position of strategic dominance along the first island chain.

security demands that China must control those seas and have unimpeded access to the Western Pacific, which requires breaching and ideally dominating the island chain. Their concern is that hostile powers could use the island chain to blockade or mount an offensive against China, which relies on sea links for international trade and energy security. They also recall that China's colonial-era invaders attacked from the sea.

At the time of writing, each of the main territories along the chain – Japan, Taiwan and the Philippines – has the United States as its military backstop. Ambiguously in the case of Taiwan, less so in the case of Japan and the Philippines, which are joined to the US by mutual-defense treaties. Once again, the narrative asserts, it is the presence of the US that ultimately blocks the People's Republic of China from achieving its objectives.

There are good security reasons for the US to want to preserve the status quo along the first island chain and retain its leading role in the Asia-Pacific, but from a PRC perspective there are better reasons for China to need to re-establish dominance in the region, and that entails changing the status quo. Current trends appear to favour China in this respect. A point must surely come, from China's perspective, where the once immoveable object yields to the newly irresistible force, allowing China to contest control of the first island chain directly with Japan, Taiwan and the Philippines, without the threat of US intervention. On the other hand, the PRC's leaders are well aware that the anticipated geopolitical dividend of their country's ascent may never materialize. There is a view amongst many economists that China's vaulting growth of the past four decades is unsustainable, maybe critically so for the ruling party. Furthermore, Japan, Vietnam and other Asian nations have their own reasons for resisting Chinese domination and will seek to do so with or without US leadership. And Taiwan in particular, where the will of the people is overwhelmingly opposed to falling under Beijing's control, is going to be a hard nut to crack, with or without US support for the Taiwanese. All this in a world of runaway climate change and proliferating politico-environmental stresses, where fixed plans are hostage to a gathering tide of unknown unknowns.

Strategic flexibility, in this contest of maritime and territorial sovereignty, is therefore as vital for the PRC as operational flexibility was for the campaigners of the Warring States era.

Progress towards China's strategic objective must therefore be largely prudent and incremental, while also featuring moves that are stealthy and unpredictable. Thus, China seeks to maneuver the United States out of the region both directly and indirectly, accruing military and political advantage ("seeking victory through strategic dominance" – ch. 5.5) while keeping its own options open.

China does so, in the prescribed Sun Tzu manner, by exploiting friction and uncertainty to undermine the objectives of the US and undermine its alliances ("Striking against an opponent's plans is the most effective strategy; striking at his alliances is the next most effective strategy" – ch. 3.2), while stealthily imposing its will on the region and capitalizing on opportunities to advance its own agenda ("he holds formation and watches for disorder on the other side" – ch. 7.5). It tests the enemy's weak points, but in a calibrated manner so as not to trigger powerful pushback. And it will try to avoid armed conflict unless the fight can be thoroughly contained in scale, or until the chances of success are overwhelmingly in China's favour ("When we choose to do battle, the enemy has no choice but to engage... when we choose to avoid battle, there is nothing the enemy can do about it" – ch. 6.3).

For the PRC, then, the number one priority during the past

twenty years of military modernization has been to engineer a strategic dynamic that progressively weakens the US resolve to defend the status quo along the first island chain, while improving the PLA's capacity for maritime power projection to the point where a limited clash of arms, should the long-term objective require one, becomes viable.

It is the kind of approach described in the Sun Tzu treatise, in operational terms, as shaping an opponent's battle posture ("we determine the dispositions of the opposing forces" – ch. 6.4) by first controlling the strategic landscape.

The aspiration for military superiority along the maritime periphery, is articulated and alluded to in authoritative literature on PLA strategy and doctrine circulated among China's armed forces by the country's Academy of Military Science and National Defense University, as well as in strategy-setting policy directives issued by PLA and CCP leadership. Many of these writings and directives emphasize the need for the PLA to prepare for an intense, regionally contained, IT-enabled war in the maritime domain. More pertinently, that aspiration is manifested in the way that military funding has been focused during the past two decades of breakneck budgetary expansion.

The priority, from the start, was to modernize and re-equip the PLA in such a way as to neutralize the obstacle to China's ambitions posed by rival air and naval forces along the maritime periphery. The development and production of ballistic missiles was accelerated in the early 1990's, as the fastest, most cost-effective means of achieving this objective. On paper that objective has already been achieved.

In the initial phase of any major military action across the Taiwan Strait, for example, a volley from the world's largest inventory of short- and medium-range ballistic missiles, ranged along China's southeast coastal regions, could within minutes disable every enemy airbase and ground or destroy all Taiwanese, US and Japanese fighter wings within unrefuelled flying distance of the Strait, giving the PLA Air Force immediate supremacy in the skies above Taiwan.

The US Navy's surface fleet, meanwhile, would have to hastily sequester itself hundreds of kilometres beyond the first island chain, well over the horizon and far from the action, to limit the threat from China's anti-ship cruise and ballistic missiles along with the PLA Navy's large fleet of attack submarines.

If it did choose to take the fight to China, the US would have to rely for air cover on a single airbase in Guam — itself now menaced by China's increasingly accurate ballistic missiles — and on aircraft carriers stood off far out in the Pacific Ocean. Air and naval losses, during the one or two weeks it might take for the US to battle its way back into contention, would surpass anything that the country has known since World War II.

The augmentation of China's missile brigades has been accompanied by high-tech tooling-up of the PLA Air Force and Navy on a huge scale. Both now deploy state-of-the-art assets that are rapidly bringing them into quantitative — and potentially qualitative — parity with the combined equivalents of their foes along the maritime periphery. China already outnumbers the US Navy in Pacific-based submarines, and launches two new, advanced-capability submarines every year. Meanwhile the PLA's cyber war and counter-space capabilities pose a comparable level of threat to the information, surveillance, command, control and communications functions of China's potential foes, as do those of the potential foes pose to China.

All told, the US Navy can no longer throw its weight around in the region as confidently as it did during the China-Taiwan crisis of 1995/96, when it dispatched two carrier groups to Taiwan — one of which steamed defiantly up the centre of the

Strait—in response to provocative missile firings from China.

Today's PLA has enough modern hardware, and generates enough uncertainty about its red lines and its capacity for self-control in a crisis, to rule out any repeat of that particular show of power. The strategic dynamic along the maritime periphery has shifted, and is shifting still, in the PRC's favour, without the PLA yet needing to chance a direct confrontation with the old "hegemon".

On the other hand, the PLA's organizational modernization has lagged far behind its hardware upgrade. The antiquated, infantry-centric force structure of the 1990s has been streamlined, with the focus moved to maritime power projection, but inadequate standards of training, logistics and command are believed to be serious weaknesses that are only now being properly tackled.

Above all, the PLA is handicapped by its negligible institutional experience of large-scale naval operations and untested ability to conduct complex, joint operations. The relative superiority of the US and its allies in these areas would increasingly come into play in any conflict that extended much beyond an initial clash of arms.

In short, China is likely to be just as unsure of the outcome of any escalation from friction to armed conflict, in the maritime periphery, as the US and its allies. How both sides perceive the opponent's will to withstand losses, is going to be critical.

Sun Tzu advises would-be combatants to test an enemy's capabilities and resolve by probing his perimeter ("Prod him into action to study his patterns of movement.... Skirmish to test where his forces are in surplus and where they are under-strength" – ch. 6.5).

China, as the challenger, necessarily sets the pace in this respect. In the East China Sea, the maritime militias—fishing fleets drilled for paramilitary operations under PLA direction—and the China Coast Guard repeatedly test Japan's tolerance for incursions and operations around the Senkaku/Diaoyu islands.

In the South China Sea, China's maritime militia, coast guard, navy and dredging-and-construction fleet (engaged for large-scale land-reclamation and military-base-building on converted shoals and reefs) keep Vietnam and the Philippines under continual pressure to justify and preserve their claims to Exclusive Economic Zones (EEZs). In both seas, China's increasingly strident assertions of sovereignty, on the water and in the air, have prodded the United States to deploy ships and planes to the area specifically to assert internationally established rights to freedom of navigation and overflight.

As with China's other potential rivals in the East and South China Seas, the US is for the most part on the back foot. In 2016 China's claim to territorial waters across most of the South China Sea was rejected at the Permanent Court of Arbitration in the Hague, in a case brought by the Philippines, but the PRC nevertheless converted the setback into a victory of sorts. The vehemence with which the party-state rejected the findings and legitimacy of the tribunal, and by extension a significant chunk of the international rules-based order, demonstrated the strength of its resolve on its maritime claims, delighting nationalist audiences at home while sending an unmistakeable signal to external opponents about the country's determination to make the rules in its own region, regardless of international norms.

If that strength of determination gives US political and military strategists pause for thought, it is meant to. The PLA's naval and organizational capabilities may not yet be advanced enough to risk escalating beyond a skirmish with the US Navy and Air Force in disputed areas, but the fact that the US military has to allow for that possibility is a strategic gain for China. The US once again edges back, visibly questioning its own bottom line for defending the status quo along the first island chain, while the PRC again edges unquestioningly forward. China's maritime periphery becomes even less hospitable for the US military, and another degree more like the Caribbean — something of a proprietorial sea dominated by the regional superpower.

Aficionados of the Sun Tzu approach to war would recognize much that is familiar in the PRC's blend of brinksmanship and caution along the maritime periphery, its national focus on overcoming a single powerful rival, its asymmetrical force posture vis-à-vis that rival, its stealthy, peacetime accumulation of political and military advantage, and its expedient adoption and jettisoning of interstate norms in pursuit of its strategic objectives.

PRC leaders increasingly appear to think and act like rulers of a 4th-century-BC Warring State, and it would seem that they have fashioned a grand strategy against the United States on that basis, without the US apparently quite recognizing that this is the case.

Taking Taiwan by strategy
Taiwan, more than any other state, knows what it is to live under sustained strategic pressure from the People's Republic of China, and its experience offers valuable insight into how today's political and military planners in Beijing put their familiarity with Sun Tzu, and the Warring States paradigm, into practice.

Taiwan is around 250 miles in length and lies smack in the middle of the first island chain, blocking China's direct access to the Pacific and forcing its Navy and Air Force through channels to the south and to the north. The island also dominates the southern trade lanes to Japan and the northern approach to the Philippines, and in Sun Tzu campaign terms would be classed as a junction zone—"an area where the approaches to three principalities intersect", from which the army that claims it "stands to dominate in every direction" (ch. 11.1).

If the perimeter of US dominion is ever to be rolled back across the ocean, freeing China to reclaim its regional primacy in line with the promises of the China Dream and the demands of the Patriotic Education campaign, then that junction zone will have to be brought under Beijing's control. Achieving that goal, by military and non-military means, is the PRC's top geostrategic priority.

In addition to its strategic importance for the PRC, the island also plays a central role in the domestic mythology of the CCP regime, the stories by which the Party rallies people to the cause of nationalism and buttresses its own legitimacy as the country's sovereign authority.

The stories tell of how Taiwan, part of Chinese territory since ancient times, was carved off by Japan in 1895, then briefly returned at the end of World War II before being stolen away again in 1949, this time by Chiang Kai-shek under US protection. Since then, the American military threat has kept the island apart from the rest of China. But despite those long years of foreign-imposed separation, the story maintains, the people on both sides of the Taiwan Strait are compatriots bound by blood. Restoring Taiwan to the embrace of the ancestral homeland, as the CCP promises, will complete China's territorial integrity, bringing closure to the Chinese Civil War and the Hundred Years of National Humiliation that preceded it.

This narrative, in its historical aspect, glosses over some problematic facts. China's Nationalist and Communist leaders only discovered Taiwan's strategic value and began laying claim to the island in the late 1930s, having previously recognized its status as a Japanese colony and/or advocated its independence from Japan. And back in the late seventeenth century, when court officials first proposed annexing Taiwan, the emperor had dismissed the idea, describing it as an "inconsequential place beyond the sea" and writing that: "taking it would be no gain, not taking it would be no loss". Three centuries earlier, the massive expeditionary fleets of Admiral Zheng He, which criss-crossed the seas of South East Asia and sailed as far as East Africa, simply bypassed Taiwan without a mention, taking no tribute from its indigenous kingdoms and leaving no trace.

Also absent from the CCP narrative is the diversity of Taiwan's cultural and ethnic heritage, the still-raw legacy of repression under the KMT after 1945, and the paradigm-shifting impact of the Taiwanese people's political journey during the past three decades, from authoritarian one-party rule to democratic elections and civil society. The reality of today's Taiwan, and its relationship with the landmass across the Strait, is more complex than the CCP's narrative would suggest.

Nevertheless, the narrative supplies a rationale for China's creeping campaign to take control of the island, which in turn serves the geostrategic objective of punching a hole through the middle of the first island chain, and helps to support the CCP's position of power.

By necessity, the campaign to take Taiwan has been mostly one of patience, subtlety and stealth. Despite having sixty times the population of Taiwan, mainland China has so far been the "weaker" party in terms of its capacity to seize Taiwan by armed force. The challenges of mounting an invasion across ninety-plus miles of difficult sea, against a heavily populated and (theoretically) well-defended island, require the attacker to start with a higher ratio of military superiority than the PLA has hitherto been able to muster, even before factoring in potential US intervention.

As a self-contained redoubt, the island presents China with the same kind of challenge that walled cities presented armies in the Warring States period — the possibility of a lengthy, costly siege with a high risk of failure. And as Sun Tzu makes clear, this is a situation to be avoided. "The rule is: attack walled cities only when there is no alternative" (ch. 3.2).

Lacking the wherewithal to overwhelm the island by sheer force, China has defaulted to the strategic principles articulated in the *Sun-tzu* and other Warring States treatises — accumulating advantage across the full scope of cross-Strait relations, minimizing the risk that any decisive clash of arms would entail, being prudent and pragmatic as well as flexible and unpredictable, and settling for small, near-term sacrifices where those support the long-term strategic objective.

In the few instances where the PRC has resorted to overt military measures against Taiwan, those measures have, since 1958 at least, been displays of resolve rather than any genuine attempt to secure a military objective. During the summer of 1958, there were constant artillery bombardments and air-to-air combat between the PLA and their Nationalist counterparts on and around the small islands of Kinmen and Matsu, just offshore from the Chinese mainland, but they petered out into an arrangement by which the PLA shelled military zones on Kinmen on alternate days, while the defenders returned fire on the days in between — both sides taking care not to hit anyone. After a few years the explosives were replaced with propaganda leaflets, but the shelling continued.

Symbolism similarly characterized the missile "tests" of 1995 and 1996, when the PLA fired ballistic missiles into the sea just off Taiwan's main shipping ports, initially to express fury at then-president Lee Teng-hui's perceived encouragement for Taiwan independence during a visit to the US, and then as a direct warning (which backfired) to the Taiwanese electorate not to choose Lee in the presidential election.

There have been other, lesser spikes of activity in the years since. PLA Air Force sorties across the centre line of the Taiwan Strait, which Taiwan's fighter pilots do not reciprocate, are now so common that they attract no public attention. Similarly with intrusive reconnaissance by PLA Navy submarines, which Taiwan's navy can do no more than cautiously monitor. The PLA periodically conducts large-scale amphibious assault exercises in conditions designed to simulate an attack on Taiwan or its offshore islands, and broadcasts the footage on Chinese television, while satellite imagery, available on the Internet, shows a full-scale mock-up of Taiwan's Presidential Palace along with the surrounding blocks of central Taipei (including a replica of the Taipei First Girls' High School) in a military zone in the drylands of northwest China, where PLA special operations troops apparently practise decapitation attacks on the Taiwan government. And for decades now, but particularly since 1996, there has been a steady drumbeat of threats from PRC leaders and spokespeople warning that China "reserves the right" to use force against Taiwan, and will counter moves towards independence with "non-peaceful means" — threats which are backed with an increasingly credible arsenal of air, naval and missile weaponry manifestly targeting Taiwan.

Interestingly, however, the PLA has yet to develop or acquire the full airlift and amphibious assault capability it would need for a conventional invasion of Taiwan.

If the PLA seems to be prevaricating, it's not because it is unwilling to open fire. Since 1958 it has fought border wars with the USSR and India, and in 1979 it sacrificed between twenty and thirty thousand Chinese troops, by Western estimates, in a shambolic invasion of Vietnam. Yet all the while, it has managed to hold fire on Taiwan—that "core issue" over which the CCP frequently declares that it is willing to go to war.

Even allowing for the real-world consequences of threats, simulated attacks, missile batteries and a rapid build-up of air and naval assault capabilities, it is evident that the CCP and PLA have, for the past six decades, cautiously avoided precipitating a decisive engagement across the Taiwan Strait. Instead, their priority has been to convey enough resolve to Taiwan's leaders and public to deter them from going it alone as a new, non-China state, but not so much as to back them into a corner and panic them into doing just that anyway. As Sun Tzu notes, it is better to "leave a gap for an army that you have surrounded" (ch. 7.6) rather than forcing it into an attritional last-ditch defense.

Beijing has settled for the practical objective of preventing "Taiwan independence" in the short term, while attempting to engineer circumstances—generating strategic dominance, in Sun Tzu terms—by which to eventually compel "reunification".

As we know from Sun Tzu, when there is a critical threat to your survival—as the CCP appears to believe Taiwan's permanent detachment from China would threaten its own survival—you bend all your strength to the task of eliminating that threat, and you do so in ways that are pragmatic, flexible, stealthy, and unpredictable. You may be crafty and ambitious, but you do not permit yourself to be rash, or intemperate, or display any other quality that weakens your ability to prevail. "A ruler should never mobilize for war in a fit of rage. A general should never attack in anger" (ch. 12.4). Instead you conduct a cool-headed, scientific assessment of the situation on both sides, and use whatever time is available to accumulate military and non-military advantages over the designated enemy.

Sun Tzu reminds us that if you get the groundwork right, minimizing risk and maximizing gain, you may manage to "force an opposing army to submit without battle" (ch. 3.1), but you must nevertheless be ready to fight when opportunity or necessity requires it. You win by first striking at the opponent's plans and alliances, before resorting to a military offensive, or, as the last option, attacking his fortified cities. The initial, non-kinetic phase of conflict may stretch over years, but you will be using this same period to prepare for the kinetic phase. By the time battle becomes inevitable, you will have arranged things such that that the odds of victory are overwhelmingly in your favour. "A winning force first secures victory, then goes into battle" (ch. 4.2).

So, how well is the PRC doing? Steady accumulation of advantage, would certainly describe how the PRC's strategy appears from a Taiwan perspective. Its military posture towards the island increasingly evokes that Sun Tzu image for realizing strategic dominance: like "drawing taut a crossbow" (ch. 5.3).

The US withdrew its forces and was eased out of its formal defense commitment to Taiwan in the 1970s following the Nixon-Mao détente. In recent years, Chinese pressure on the US and other countries, combined with eight years of genuflecting to the CCP by a pro-unification KMT administration on Taiwan up until 2016, has so restricted the sale of defensive weaponry to the island that Taiwan's armed forces seem, in some respects, to be frozen in time.

Across the Strait, meanwhile, the PLA consumes the second largest military budget in the world (its annual increment alone is greater than Taiwan's entire military budget), and most of that budget is geared to the principal contingency that China wants to be able to fight for—the battle for Taiwan.

Taiwan's airpower is spearheaded by a fleet of 1980s-vintage F-16 fighters, complemented by outdated indigenous fighters and soon-to-be retired Mirages. The F-16s are being refurbished in batches, and fewer than seventy of them are available on the island at any time. China, meanwhile, has several hundred modern fighters based within un-refuelled flight distance of Taiwan, along with newly-developed stealth models due to enter service by 2020.

While Taiwan relies on a pair of forty-year-old submarines (patrolling one at a time) for undersea operations, backed up with two WW2 relics used for training, the PLA Navy deploys 30-40 modern submarines out of a fleet of 70, and is adding to that number by two per year through to 2030.

And while Taiwan has missile defenses capable of intercepting a limited number of warplanes and cruise missiles, it cannot realistically shield itself against China's arsenal of ballistic missiles, 1,500 of which currently target Taiwan's critical military and civil infrastructure.

In fact, the military balance across the Strait has shifted to such an extent in recent years that the PLA could already, if it chose, demolish Taiwan's defensive strategy in a single night of stand-off attacks, neutralizing Taiwan's air and naval bases, overwhelming its air defenses and crippling its command-and-control infrastructure through a combination of asymmetrical kinetic attacks and cyber war. Whether that would be a rational move and what China would do next, are open questions — transparency is not part of the CCP lexicon — but the kinetic and cyber capacity is there, and the potential for Beijing to act in a non-rational way is credible. This influences Taiwan's cross-Strait political and military calculus, just as it is meant to.

Equally important, that potential for Taiwan to succumb to a knockout hit days before effective assistance could be rallied from across the Pacific, influences the political and military calculus of Taiwan's ambivalent ally, the US.

Being able to pose a viable military threat against Taiwan has earned China valuable influence over decision-making in both Taipei and Washington, and maintaining ambiguity about its red lines has helped it to preserve and deepen that influence during the past sixty years. Had China tried to convert threats into substantive action at any point during that period, it most likely would have wrecked the programme, dragging America back into the Strait and prompting Taiwan to permanently decouple.

As Sun Tzu reiterates, war is in large part a discipline of waiting and watching, tracking the adversary and adjusting to circumstances until the strategic landscape is firmly in your favour, "shadow[ing] the enemy for hundreds of miles before eliminating his high command" (ch. 11.10).

In a similar vein, China has accumulated sizeable economic leverage over Taiwan since the two sides opened to each other in the 1990s then jointly acceded to the WTO. China's GDP was roughly double Taiwan's in 1990, but by 2015 it had grown to twenty times greater. Taiwan, whose economy depends on foreign trade, ships just over a quarter of its exports to its giant neighbour — significant exposure when the major trade partner is a potentially hostile power. Some 80% of Taiwan's accumulated foreign direct investment (FDI) is believed to be in China, and a million or more Taiwanese businesspeople and professionals live and work there. China has plenty of options for hurting Taiwan with economic sanctions, if it chooses.

As with the military threat, however, China's direct economic leverage over Taiwan has to date been more useful held in reserve than actively applied. The cascading consequences of economic dislocation are even less easy to predict than those of armed conflict. On the face of things, Taiwan is vulnerable because it is more dependent on the relationship than China is. But the opposite may also be true. Taiwan is indeed susceptible to action against its strategic industries, its financial markets, its property sector, and its manufacturers based in China, but it also has generations of experience as a scrappy outsider creating profitable niches for itself in global supply chains, and this is an advantage which keeps its economy flexible and resilient.

China, on the other hand, for all its economic mass, has relied on a handful of wealthy coastal provinces as its engine of GDP growth over the past three decades. Those same provinces are deeply intertwined with Taiwanese industries and would pay a disproportionately heavy price for any damage to the Taiwan economy. The knock-on effects could open up political and economic fissures in China and turn people against the regime – a gamble that the CCP has so far chosen to avoid.

The PRC's long-term objective has been better served, so far, by applying economic pressure selectively and in support of a broader political approach. In recent years, that has meant wielding carrots and sticks against targeted sectors of the population to register imperial favour or displeasure, exploiting fault lines in Taiwan society and sowing confusion about China's intentions.

China's punitive measures against targeted groups and individuals in Taiwan tend to backfire when too blatant, provoking ire and rallying Taiwanese around the flag. By and large, however, they conform with the CCP's long-established pattern for applying political and psychological pressure – co-opting those Taiwanese who are influential and amenable, shunning and undermining those who are not – and impressing on all Taiwanese the notion that their personal livelihood and national prospects depend to a large degree on showing deference to China.

The message being conveyed to people in Taiwan is that they and their once-vigorous "Asian Tiger" economy are insignificant and isolated, dependent on China's goodwill and unable to act in the international sphere without China's say-so. More generally, the PRC needs them to internalize a sense that the cross-Strait dynamic is evolving in one direction only, and will continue doing so until Taiwan is subsumed under the banner of the unified republic.

That process of forcing the Taiwanese to internalize the inevitability of Taiwan's incorporation into China, is advanced by a psyops-type package of policies and processes which the PLA calls "the three warfares". Like their earlier iteration in the form of political warfare—which the Communists and Nationalists waged against each other for decades—the three warfares aim for military advantage by non-kinetic means, in particular by strategic use of information to shape perceptions, to intimidate, and ultimately to break an adversary's will. In effect, the three warfares weaponize the flow of information during peacetime, exploiting the relative inattention of opponents during early phases of confrontation, well before the threshold of kinetic war is reached.

As directed against Taiwan, the three warfares described in the PLA literature are:

(a) psychological warfare, to influence the collective mood and morale of people in Taiwan and further afield;

(b) media warfare, to create a perception that the general public solidly backs the PRC approach to Taiwan; and

(c) legal warfare, for instituting new statutory norms to buttress China's position on Taiwan.

The essence of the three warfares approach is to dominate domestic and international discourse on Taiwan to such a degree that it becomes practically impossible to think outside the boundaries of China's narrative. Plans for Taiwan that are not predicated on the island's eventual absorption into China, become first un-utterable, and then unthinkable. Allies cannot muster the will to rouse themselves in Taiwan's cause, lacking a plausible rationale for doing so. In this way, the battle is won in the collective mind of any would-be defenders, before China has to deploy military resources in anger and risk besieging the island.

From a Sun Tzu perspective, China's campaign to dominate the discourse has had some success in Taiwan, particularly among those sectors of society still tied in with the networks of political and financial patronage through which the KMT kept itself in power for decades. Compliant media organizations and industry groups in Taiwan have dutifully done their bit to shape public opinion in terms that favour China's—and their own—interests, while elements of Taiwan's old-guard moneyed elite, including a sizable proportion of the island's retired senior military officers, have welcomed the CCP's blandishments and turned themselves into cheerleaders for China's narrative of inevitable "reunification" with Taiwan.

In the international sphere, meanwhile, Taiwan's already precarious national status (it remains excluded from the UN, at China's insistence, and is formally recognized by only a handful of diplomatic allies) worsens every time that an official Taiwanese delegation attends a multinational gathering or event under one of the awkward designations imposed on it by the PRC, such as "Chinese Taipei" or "Taiwan, Province of China". Year by year the precedent deepens, in international law and in the eyes of the world, that Taiwan accepts submission to PRC sovereignty.

This perception is reinforced by the One China framework within which Zhou Enlai expertly tied the hands of President Nixon—and subsequent US administrations—in the 1972 Shanghai Communique. The resulting One-China policy, by which the United States acknowledged but neither supported nor challenged the PRC's position on Taiwan (and under which it de-recognized Taiwan's "Republic of China" government in 1978), is interpreted within China as an implicit endorsement of the PRC's claim to sovereignty over the island. That *policy* was later globalized by China into what it calls the One-China *principle*, under which the nations of the world are relentlessly pressured into accepting the PRC claim to Taiwan.

Little by little, the space in which to voice or conceive of a non-China narrative for Taiwan, shrinks.

Meanwhile, China's fierce reaction to any hint of acknowledgement for Taiwan's *de facto* separate identity incrementally nudges international law—as practised in East Asia, at least—away from post-WWII principles of sovereign equality and the right of peoples to self-determination, and instead towards a more hierarchical, imperial conception of interstate relations.

The CCP has even passed legislation committing it to use force against Taiwan under certain circumstances, including at any time that the CCP concludes the path to unification has been closed off. This is an example of legal warfare, within the three warfares strategy, in that it provides the PLA with a fig leaf of statutory justification for any future "defensive" attack on Taiwan.

In sum, China has actively applied the three warfares approach to pressure people, both on and off Taiwan, into accepting the PRC's strategic narrative and thus its right to pursue the objective of taking control of the island. If all goes to plan, China will "overawe with such authority" (ch. 11.8) that the Taiwanese will not rally to their own defense, and the island's potential allies will be discouraged from intervening at a time of crisis.

The longer that military and economic trends in China's favour persist, the more it seems that Taiwan's people and institutions could eventually accept their assigned role in China's strategic narrative and resign themselves to matters being resolved on Beijing's terms. The PRC's stunning rise to wealth and power in recent years has reinforced the impression that the CCP has history on its side. Who is to say, then, that the party's long-game, Sun Tzu-style approach to Taiwan won't eventually pay off, with or without a military end-game?

Yet there are other significant trends afoot, even aside from the military challenges of taking Taiwan, which argue for a different outcome.

In particular, Taiwan's increasingly embedded experience of democratic elections and peaceful transfers of power, combined with a surge of progressive, Taiwan-first national identity among young Taiwanese, suggest that the island's people will not voluntarily yield to Beijing's control.

Meanwhile, across the Strait, the party-state has been tightening political restrictions just as the country's rising middle class has been moving in the other direction, towards civil society and universal values (which the CCP derides as "Western" values). The Party appears increasingly out of step with the mainstream mood of the people it governs, and this puts in question the amount of domestic support that the regime could rely on in a time of all-out crisis — such as the crisis that would result from any attempt by China to seize control of Taiwan against the will of the Taiwanese people.

There are also doubts about how well China is implementing its strategy for Taiwan, and whether or not it can even be said to have a coherent strategy.

The goal — taking control of Taiwan — is fixed, and the underlying strategic principles, honed through over 2,000 years of Chinese military culture, are virtually immutable. But several of the policies that China has adopted along the way in pursuit of that goal, have been tactical failures — most notably the attempt to win over Taiwan with the "one country, two systems" formula. "One country, two systems" was originally designed in the 1980s for Taiwan, with the intention of smoothing the island's eventual, consensual absorption into the PRC.

The formula was adapted for Hong Kong, and its successful implementation there was expected to offer a reassuring model for people in Taiwan. At the core of "one country, two systems" was a guarantee to extend the enclave's British-style rule of law, with its independent judiciary, beyond the 1997 handover. The arrangement worked more or less as intended, to begin with, but since 2012 the PRC authorities have increasingly been tampering with it. In 2014, a showdown over China's imposed method for selecting the territory's chief executive, led to mass protests — the Umbrella Movement — which blocked city-centre streets for weeks on end, while 2015 saw the bizarre abduction of five Hong Kong booksellers (scurrilous publications of theirs were thought to have upset powerful CCP figures, but they had otherwise committed no offence under Hong Kong law) by PRC public security agencies. The abductions, which took place shortly before a general election in Taiwan, did no favours for the prospects of the Beijing-leaning KMT in that election and finished off any credibility that might have remained for the "one country, two systems" formula in Taiwan.

Beijing's biggest obstacle in Taiwan is no longer the military or government, but the mindset and aspirations of the island's 24 million people. Surveys indicate that while a small and dwindling proportion of Taiwan's citizenry might countenance a future being directly governed from Beijing, a large majority would not.

It was not supposed to be like this. Back in the days of "the two Chiangs" (Chiang Kai-shek and Chiang Ching-kuo, the father and son rulers of Taiwan from 1949-1988), when the template for cross-strait relations was set, both sides were one-party states. China's strategic approach was accordingly predicated on pressuring the island's political, military and economic elites to generate the decisions that Beijing required.

The rest of Taiwan's citizens, in this scenario, were like the "common people" passingly alluded to in the *Sun-tzu* and other texts of its era — an undifferentiated mass susceptible to shrewd manipulation by the governing authorities.

Nowadays, however, Taiwan is a feisty, open society, and its people are key players in the island's political mix, introducing myriad complications of a kind never envisaged by Sun Tzu.

The three warfares approach has gone some way towards advancing China's cause in Taiwan, but so far no amount of strategic planning has managed to keep up with the shifting demands and expectations of people in what has become a diverse, dynamic, fast-maturing democracy.

The only sure way to win over voters is to offer what a plurality of them want. At present, Beijing will not do that for Taiwan. It could conceivably impose its will by engineering a coup, or by blockading or invading the island, but any one of these actions would trigger a chain of uncontrollable consequences. Does Sun Tzu have an answer for China's predicament? Do even policy hawks in Beijing look forward to the prospect of subduing Taiwan by force then ruling by terror?

The CCP might well gain control of Taiwan, dominion over the seas within the first island chain, and a proprietorial gateway to Pacific, while settling a bunch of historical scores along the way, but those gains would come at incalculable cost, for both China and the world.

The *Sun-tzu*, if it has anything to teach the CCP — and bearing in mind that the Warring States "world-under-heaven" is not necessarily a good analogue for even East Asia, let alone Planet Earth in the 21ˢᵗ century — it is probably that invasion or coerced annexation of Taiwan are not currently worth the risk and the costs.

Sun Tzu's "clear-sighted sovereign and worthy general" (ch. 13.1) would run their calculations in the national altar-hall, and pragmatically conclude that while Taiwan cannot be decisively won, at least at present, its continued autonomy does not, for the time being, critically threaten the existence of China's party-state.

"Do not move unless it is to your advantage," advises the treatise. "Do not deploy troops unless it brings gains. Do not give battle unless the situation is critical" (ch. 12.3).

In the meantime, therefore, Sun Tzu counsels the CCP to continue shaping the strategic landscape to suit its objectives, preventing Taiwan's graduation from *de facto* to *de jure* independence and progressively cramping Taiwan's space for maneuver — but not so obviously as to trigger determined pushback. The Taiwan people, for their part, may continue cementing their identity as citizens of an autonomous democracy, but also taking care not to antagonize the thin-skinned regime across the Strait.

On the downside for Taiwan, this means enduring an indefinite extension of today's state of affairs in which China is free to boss and belittle it, while the world to one extent or another turns a blind eye. The CCP, for its part, will have to endure continued uncertainty about its own capacity for remaining in power *without* achieving that strategic objective of taking control of Taiwan.

This would be a less-than-ideal outcome for both parties in the dispute, but better — pending future evolution of the strategic landscape — than any currently feasible alternative.

As both sides may remind themselves: "Victory can be known in advance, but it cannot be forced" (ch. 4.1).

———— ∾ ————

The principles and approaches outlined in the *Sun-tzu* and transmitted to the present day in the form of a kind of strategic second nature in China's body politic, so far appear to have served the PRC party-state well. The regime somehow survived the self-inflicted catastrophes of the Mao era, and has guided China from weakness to strength in the years since then, cautiously focussing on maximizing long-term advantage while minimizing risk and cost along the way.

Throughout that process, the CCP has fostered a deliberative, risk-averse, siege-mentality type of national mindset, while priming the Chinese people for a return to an all-out war-footing whenever the regime deems it necessary.

The immediate precedent for this approach was the CCP's formative experience as a small, vulnerable guerrilla force in a remote region of northwest China, where it based itself in the 1930s and 1940s while preparing for the final phase of Civil War (1946-1949) against the Nationalist-run Chinese government. But a deeper precedent was set by strategies of Cao Cao and his counterparts in the third century, and the campaigns of the warring states in the third to fifth centuries BC, and the tales of King Gou Jian of Yue and similar canny, determined, patient combatants throughout Chinese history, all exemplifying aspects of the strategic paradigm outlined by Sun Tzu.

Whether that paradigm will serve the PRC and its CCP masters well in the years ahead, remains to be seen. In Sun Tzu terms, to be a state is to be at war. "War is the defining function of the state" (ch. 1.1). States must battle for survival, and that is that. But in the 21st century, with nuclear arsenals on standby and staggering environmental and social challenges ahead, no major state will survive a war of attrition. There can be no Sun Tzu-type "victory" against a military peer.

One way or another China is going to have to find new strategies for squaring away its differences with the US and Japan, new tactics for developing its maritime periphery, and new narratives for its relationship with Taiwan. And China's ruling Communist Party, if it truly wants to serve the Chinese people, is going to have to turn away from the Warring States period and find a new paradigm.

As the old pragmatist who was Sun Tzu—whoever he may have been—would surely agree, we can no longer expect the Sun-tzu to answer all the strategic challenges of the "world under heaven".

PART TWO

THE SUN-TZU

TRANSLATOR'S NOTE

THE WORK OF TRANSLATING a world classic begins inevitably in the shadow of previous translations. There have been around a dozen reputable translations of Sun Tzu into English since the first, by Captain E. F. Calthrop, was published in Tokyo in 1905, and each manages, in its own unique way, to bridge the gap between the ancient text and its readers in modern English.

For this translation—which takes as its base text the standard edition by Sun Hsing-yen (1752-1818), modified in the light of recent scholarship—I aimed to echo the pragmatic, methodical tone of the original. This is a significant feature of the treatise and gives Sun Tzu's approach the character of a "science" more than an "art", but it has often been downplayed or missed in previous translations.

Like any translator, I try to interpret and express the sense of words and phrases as accurately and objectively as possible. There are plenty of points in Sun Tzu where contemporary translators, in common with centuries of Chinese scholars before them, disagree on the meaning of individual words and phrases, and have to rely on subjective interpretation. The translator's challenge is to be aware of that tendency towards subjectivity, taking care not to distort the original meaning by interpreting too freely, at the same time as being confident in, and able to account for, one's own necessarily subjective choices and decisions.

The five examples below are chosen to illustrate and account for a handful of the significant, subjective choices made in the course of producing the current translation.

1. The opening line of Sun Tzu, after the formulaic "Sun Tzu states...", reads: "War is the defining function of the state. It is a realm of life-and-death struggle. It is how nations perish or persist" (ch. 1.1).

In Chinese, the first of those three short statements begins with the character *bing* (兵), meaning armed conflict, but also military matters in general, by extension from the character's earliest meanings of weapon, and soldier. *Bing* announces the statement's topic, and that topic is then commented on, in four characters: *guo-zhi-da-shi*. *Guo* (國), meaning a state, principality, or kingdom; *zhi* (之), a possessive marker; *da* (大) meaning big, grand; and *shi* (事) meaning business, matter, affair of state.

For this statement, a translator might begin by jotting down something like: "War: a major issue for the state"—and then rewrite as necessary.

In some of the previous translations, the statement is rendered as follows:

> The art of war is of vital importance to the state (Giles, 1910)

> Military action is important to the nation (Cleary, 1988)

> War is a vital matter of state (Ames, 1993)

In each case we gain the sense that war, for all its significance, is perhaps one among several important areas of consideration for the state.

One translation takes a different tack, however:

Warfare is the greatest affair of state (Sawyer, 1994)

Sawyer's interpretation of the statement tallies closely with how I read it. That character *shi*, in this context, does not refer to any old matter, but an essential obligation of the state – a grand, official undertaking by which the state legitimizes its existence – and *da* does not simply mean "big" but "the biggest". We can infer this because the expression "*guo-zhi-da-shi*" was in circulation well before Sun Tzu, and was used to describe state-level sacrificial rites, along with the ritual observances necessary as part of national preparations for battle.[1] By redefining *guo-zhi-da-shi* and limiting its scope to the realm of warfare alone, Sun Tzu bluntly asserts the *raison d'etre* of the Warring States. Waging war was, by Sun Tzu's day, the *only* way for states to survive and succeed. It was the very activity that made a state a state. Hence, in this translation, "the defining function of the state".

2. Perhaps the most commonly quoted line of Sun Tzu appears as follows:

To subdue the enemy without fighting is the acme of skill (Griffith, 1963)

Ultimate excellence lies /...in defeating the enemy / Without ever fighting (Minford, 2002)

Causing the enemy forces to submit without a battle is the most excellent approach (Mair, 2007)

---

1   The state-level rituals of sacrifice and warfare were defined as *guo-zhi-da-shi* in a statement attributed to the Lord of Liu in 577 BC, and recorded in the canonical work *Zuo Zhuan*.

This idea is often abbreviated to "winning without fighting", and cited approvingly, both in English and Chinese, as evidence of Sun Tzu's essentially peaceful intentions. What the original text depicts, however, is a particular action, *qu* (屈) — meaning to subdue, or subjugate, or force to submit — directed against a particular object, *ren-zhi-bing* (人之兵) — meaning another party's soldiers or army — in a context of *bu-zhan* (不戰) — literally "not engaging in battle".

Sun Tzu does not suggest that the process of subduing the other party should be benign, only that it is best done without damaging one's own forces. The victorious commander may even liquidate the opposing army once it is under his control. The essential thing is that he gains that control without risking his assets in a destructive clash of arms.

To properly convey this idea, it seems important to retain the image of that object, *bing* — a menacing body of armed men — rather than subsuming it into the generic term "enemy". It is also worth capturing the coercive implications of *qu* in this context, where it means forcing the other party to submit on your terms, rather than simply generalizing it into the notion of "winning" or "defeating".

The result, in this translation, is: "The military ideal is to force an opposing army to submit without battle" (ch. 3.1).

3. Another statement of Sun Tzu's, often cited in translation, is this:

> If you know the enemy and know yourself, you need not fear the result of a hundred battles (Giles, 1910)

> He who knows the enemy and himself / Will never in a hundred battles be at risk (Ames, 1993)

CHRISTOPHER MACDONALD

> Know the enemy and know yourself; in a hundred battles
> you will never be defeated (Yuan Shibing's translation of
> Tao Hanzhang, 1987)

The first part of the couplet, in the original, reads *zhi-bi-zhi-ji*. *Zhi* (知), meaning know, understand; *bi* (彼), meaning them, their, other; *zhi* (知), know, understand; and *ji* (己) oneself. Previous English-language translations all render the key character *zhi* as "know", and wrap it in neat phrasing that evokes the classical Greek maxim rendered in English as "know thyself".

The word "know" spans a field of meaning in English, just as the character *zhi* does in modern and classical Chinese. The two overlap, but are not identical. In this context, the sense from Sun Tzu is that a commander needs to be fully aware of both sides' capability and capacity for battle. Also implied is the value of having a good grasp of both sides' plans, priorities, hopes and fears. Modern Chinese versions of the classical text favour the Chinese word for "understand" at this point, and I followed their example. At the same time I felt obliged to elaborate, to the minimum degree possible, just what it is about both sides that one is expected to "understand".

I also had to decide how to construct the English sentence. As in the three examples above, previous translations of this statement are equally split between those which begin "If you...", those which begin "One who/he who...", and those which open with a solidly imperative "Know the enemy...". Contemporary versions in Mandarin vernacular incline towards a condition-consequence structure, in the form: "understanding X, means being able to Y", which I adopted to produce the following: "When one understands the condition of the opposition and the condition of one's own side, one fights a hundred battles without ever facing defeat" (ch. 3.7).

I think readers would prefer something more succinct. In my

translation, the four neatly balanced characters which comprise the first part of the couplet in classical Chinese, *zhi-bi-zhi-ji*, have been transformed into an inelegant string of 15 English words. The compact symmetry of the original is lost in translation.

Yet each of those four characters in the original embraces a field of meaning that would have been instantly accessible to early readers and students of the text, and would have provided them with fertile material for analysis and discussion – especially given that the text was expected to be taught and read out loud. The concern is that without added elaboration in English, those fields of potential meaning fall away.

In short, this couplet awaits a better translation, one that more effectively bridges the gap between the taut, expressive structure of the original, and the need to capture, for contemporary readers in English, a broader semantic range than can be conveyed by the unmodified use of the words "know", or "understand".

4. An important character, which appears 24 times in Sun Tzu and is an interesting challenge for any translator, is dao (道). As discussed in Part One, *dao* was originally a term for road or path, which subsequently branched into a range of figurative usages, including the metaphysical concept of the Way.

In the opening chapter of Sun Tzu, *dao* is first on the list of critical factors by which to assess and analyse the relative advantages of the opposing parties in war. Several previous translations render the character at this point as "the way" or "the Way" or "the Tao". "Moral influence" and "moral law" are used by others, and in one authoritative translation *dao* is rendered as "politics". Sun Tzu, in Chapter 1, then defines *dao* as that which "rallies people behind their leader and motivates them to stake their lives for him, undaunted by danger", and asks his readers to consider "Which of the opposing rulers has [*dao*] on his side?"

The same translation issue arises in Chapter 4, in a statement which directly links the quality of a commander's *dao* with his ability to be victorious in war:

> The expert in using the military builds upon the way (tao) and holds fast to military regulations, and thus is able to be the arbiter of victory and defeat (Ames, 1993)

> The Skilful Strategist / Cultivates / The Way / And preserves / The Law; / Thus he is master / Of victory and defeat. (Minford, 2002)

> Those skilled in war cultivate their policies and strictly adhere to the laws and regulations. Thus it is in their power to achieve success. (Yuan/Tao, 1987)

Judging by the definition of *dao* in Chapter 1, and the context provided in Chapter 4, the text appears to invoke both moral *and* political authority. The two are interwoven after all—even the least moral of political leaders claims to serve a just cause—so at these points in the text I opted to expand on the character as follows: "Which of the opposing rulers has moral and political authority on his side?" (ch. 1.3), and: "A great commander cultivates his moral and political authority and champions institutional order. In this way, he alone is capable of determining the military outcome" (ch. 4.2).

This is one translator's subjective interpretation, however, and Sun Tzu doesn't give us much more information to go on. He frames his point using the broadest of concepts (not to mention a Chinese character which happens to be one of the most difficult to translate into English) then leaves it with readers to apply that concept how they will.

5. Another key character in Sun Tzu which taxes translators,

is *shi* (勢), discussed in some detail in Part One.

Sun Tzu's commentators and translators agree that the concept, as applied in the treatise, describes a sense of momentum or potential energy in the course of conflict, by which one side gains, or stands to gain, overwhelming military advantage. *Shi* is a dynamic phenomenon, difficult to isolate and dependent on innumerable situational factors, but its impact in war is unmistakeable.

Sun Tzu captures the meaning of *shi* with a number of striking analogies and metaphors. *Shi* is "like a torrent, forceful enough to tumble boulders" (ch. 5.3). It is as unstoppable as "boulders rolling down the flank of a mile-high mountain" (ch. 5.5). For a commander who has maneuvered his army into the perfect position and is poised to unleash its *shi*, the experience is like "drawing taut a crossbow" (ch. 5.3).

Among previous translations, *shi* has been rendered as "energy", "potential", "momentum" "force", "strategic configuration" and "strategic advantage". That last phrase, from Ames (1993), comes closest to how I understand the term. *Shi* is both a gathering accumulation of strategic advantage, during the run-up to and early stages of conflict, and the conversion of that advantage, in the midst of battle, into overpowering facts on the ground. In this translation it appears as "strategic dominance".

Selected quotations

THE FOLLOWING are some of the more significant and better known sayings from Sun Tzu, loosely grouped by theme. Though best read in context, each offers a shortcut into the treatise's strategic and tactical philosophy. Chapter references are in brackets.

Why war?

War is the defining function of the state. (1.1)

兵者國之大事

Mind and maneuver

Warfare is all about trickery and deceit. (1.5)

兵者詭道也

When prepared for war, appear unprepared. Where deploying for battle, appear not to be deploying for battle. (1.5)

能而示之不能用而示之不用

Strike where he is undefended. Emerge where least expected. (1.5)

攻其無備出其不意

Battles generally begin with orthodox openings, but it is the unconventional move that wins the day. (5.2)

凡戰者以正合以奇勝

The ultimate in troop dispositions is to have no discernible dispositions. (6.6)
形兵之極至于無形

Military dispositions should be as fluid as water. (6.7)
兵形象水

When the enemy requests a truce out of the blue, it is a ploy. (9.3)
無約而請和者謀也

In armed conflict, what matters most is not the number of men on either side. (9.5)
兵非貴益多

In war, speed is of the essence. (11.2)
兵之情主速

The price of war

No state has ever profited from protracted war. (2.2)
兵久而國利者未之有也

Discipline

When orders are executed consistently, a commander can depend on his men and the men can depend on their commander. (9.6)
令素行者與眾相得也

Being in command

A commander who does not fully comprehend the harm caused by military action, cannot properly understand the advantages to be gained through military action. (2.2)
不盡知用兵之害者則不能盡知用兵之利也

When a commander is as concerned for his men's safety as if they were infants, they will venture with him into the deepest gorge. (10.4)
視卒如嬰兒故可與之赴深谿

When he brings the army to the brink of battle, it is as if a ladder back to the ground has been kicked away. (11.5)
帥與之期如登高而去其梯

Logistics

An astute general provisions his forces at the enemy's expense. (2.3)
智將務食於敵

Damage limitation

A state preserved intact is better than a state destroyed in war. (3.1)
全國為上破國次之

The military ideal is to force an opposing army to submit without battle. (3.1)
不戰而屈人之兵善之善者也

He maximizes the military gains though his blades remain unblunted. (3.2)
兵不頓而利可全

Avoiding sieges

The rule is: attack walled cities only when there is no alternative. (3.2)
攻城之法為不得已

Defense and offense

Being invincible is something that one decides for oneself, but it is the enemy who determines his own defeat. (4.1)

不可勝在己可勝在敵

Never rely on the opponent opting not to advance, only on one's own capacity to respond when he does. (8.4)

無恃其不來恃吾有以待也

Victory

What is prized in war is victory, not the drawn-out struggle. (2.5)

兵貴勝不貴久

A winning force first secures victory, then goes into battle. (4.2)

勝兵先勝而後求戰

Strategic dominance

The troops of a victorious army surge into battle like a flash flood crashing through a mile-deep gorge. (4.4)

勝者之戰民也若決積水于千仞之谿

A great tactician seeks victory through strategic dominance, rather than looking to others to deliver victory for him. (5.5)

善戰者求之于勢不責于人

Controlling the battlesphere

An accomplished campaigner imposes his will on the opponent rather than being imposed upon. (6.1)

善戰者致人而不致于人

Emerge where the enemy has no time to respond. Speed to
wherever least anticipated. (6.2)
出其所不趨趨其所不意

Morale

An expert commander avoids battle when the opponent's
morale is at its peak, and strikes instead when enemy troops are
tired and homesick. (7.5)
善用兵者避其銳氣擊其惰歸

Courage

Extreme situations make soldiers fearless. When there is
nowhere to run, they stand firm. (11.3)
兵士甚陷則不懼無所往則固

Patience and caution

Move only when it suits your purpose. Otherwise stay put.
(11.2 and 12.4)
合于利而動不合于利而止

A ruler should never mobilize for war in a fit of rage. A general
should never attack in anger. (12.4)
主不可以怒而興師將不可以慍而致戰

Follow through

Failing to consolidate the gains of battle is a deadly mistake.
(12.3)
戰勝攻取而不修其攻者凶

THE SUN-TZU IN TRANSLATION

THE SUN-TZU IN TRANSLATION

CHAPTER 1

ASSESSING THE CONDITIONS

"A commander who assesses conditions
in the way that I prescribe,
brings victory."

1
The defining function of the state

Sun Tzu states:

War is the defining function of the state. It is a realm of life-and-death struggle. It is how nations perish or persist.

It is imperative that this be studied and understood in depth.

2
Five factors for analysis

Analyse the situation in terms of five sets of factors, assessing the relative strength of the two sides so as to reveal the true strategic picture.

~ First, moral and political authority

~ Second, "sky"

~ Third, "ground"

~ Fourth, generalship.

~ Fifth, military organization.

Moral and political authority is what rallies people behind their leader and motivates them to stake their lives for him, undaunted by danger.

"Sky" refers to climatic conditions such as darkness and light, cold and heat, and the cycle of the seasons.

"Ground" indicates physical distances, features of the terrain, breadth of room for maneuver, and the degree of danger at any given location.

Generalship concerns a commander's intelligence, integrity,

compassion, courage, and his capacity to inspire fear
and respect.

Military organization encompasses regimental structure,
hierarchy of command and the management of logistics
and resources.

No general is unfamiliar with these five sets of factors.
Those who understand them, win wars. Those who do
not understand them, do not win wars.

So, assess the relative strength of the two sides and reveal
the true strategic picture.

3
Questions to consider

Questions to consider are:
   ~ Which of the opposing rulers has moral and political
   authority on his side?
   ~ Which side has the more able generals?
   ~ Which side has the advantages of "sky" and "ground"?
   ~ Which side has better organizational discipline?
   ~ Which side has the stronger body of troops?
   ~ Which side has the more seasoned officers and men?
   ~ Which side has the more discriminating system of
   penalties and rewards?
By this means I can forecast the outcome of the conflict.

4
Assessing conditions

A commander who assesses conditions in the way that I prescribe, brings victory. Retain him.

A commander who does not assess conditions in the way that I prescribe, brings defeat. Dismiss him.

By assessing conditions and heeding the results, one comes to assert strategic dominance, thereby strengthening one's position in every respect.

Strategic dominance is a matter of exercising control over the situation by exploiting opportunities.

_____

5
Trickery and deceit

Warfare is all about trickery and deceit.

When prepared for war, appear unprepared. Where deploying for battle, appear not to be deploying for battle.

When closing in on the enemy, appear to be far off, and when still far off appear to be closing in.

Use bait to draw the enemy out of position. When his forces are in disarray, engulf them.

If he concentrates his forces, brace for the attack. If he is too strong, take evasive action.

If the enemy is intemperate, stoke his anger. If he seems diffident, encourage him to be arrogant.

When his forces are at ease, harass them. If they are cohesive, break them up.

Strike where he is undefended. Emerge where least expected.

Strategists fashion victory from tactics such as these. Details are never revealed in advance.

_____

6
Pre-battle calculations

Where pre-battle calculations at the field temple signify victory, it is because they generate a high score. Where pre-battle calculations at the field temple do not signify victory, it is because they generate a low score.

High scores signify victory, low scores do not signify victory. It is self-evident what no score signifies.

By this means, I know in advance which side will win.

CHAPTER 2

MAKING WAR

"No state has ever profited from
protracted war."

1
Supplies and costs

Sun Tzu states:

In accordance with standard military doctrine, a campaign requires

~ 1,000 assault chariots

~ 1,000 leather-clad wagons

~ 100,000 armoured soldiers

~ Provisions for marching hundreds of miles.[1]

By the time you mobilize a 100,000-man force you will be spending upwards of a thousand gold pieces per day on miscellaneous domestic and foreign expenditures, state hospitality for allies, expensive raw materials such as resin and lacquer, and the procurement of chariots and armour.

2
Quick victory

The purpose of going to war is to win. When conflict drags on, blades go blunt and morale slumps. Sieges in particular deplete the army's strength. A lengthy campaign on foreign soil drains the nation of its wealth. Blunt weapons, demoralized men, depleted strength and exhausted supplies are vulnerabilities that foreign princes will prey on. By that point it is too late to remedy

---

1   The text refers to a "thousand-*li*" march. A *li* is equivalent to around a third of a mile.

the situation, even with support from the most astute of advisers.

Military history offers various examples of blundering haste, but none of a campaign that was "cleverly prolonged." No state has ever profited from protracted war.

A commander who does not fully comprehend the harm caused by military action, cannot properly understand the advantages to be gained through military action.

3
The economic impact of war

A great commander does not demand additional rounds of conscription. He does not need to repeatedly replenish army provisions.

On enemy soil it is right to have materiel and equipment transported from home, but for food the men should live off the land. In this way, the army will have sufficient supplies. A state beggars itself trying to provision far-off expeditionary forces. Long-distance supply lines impoverish the population back home.

Prices soar in the vicinity of the army. As prices soar, people use up their money and resources to get by. Having used up their money and resources, they are pressed for military levies. The army is depleted of strength and the people are stripped of their wealth. All across the agricultural heartland, homes are left abandoned.

Among the common people, economic consumption declines by seventy percent during war. As to state

THE SCIENCE OF WAR

expenditure, sixty percent goes on fixing broken chariots, replacing horses, and procuring armour, helmets, crossbows and bolts, halberds, shields, siege screens, draught oxen and goods wagons.

So, an astute general provisions his forces at the enemy's expense. One cartload of enemy grain is worth 20 cartloads transported from home. One barrow of enemy fodder is worth 20 barrows from home.

4
Capturing chariots

Now, soldiers have to be spurred into a rage if they are to kill the enemy. If they are required to seize resources from the enemy, however, they must be offered booty.

So, in chariot battle, once ten or more enemy chariots have been captured, reward those who took the first one. Replace the colors on the prize chariots and promptly field them as one's own. Treat the captives well and induct them into one's own ranks. This is known as augmenting one's strength while defeating the enemy.

5
Understanding the reality of war

Now, what is prized in war is victory, not the drawn-out struggle.

A commander who understands the realities of war, determines the fate of his men and keeps the nation secure.

CHAPTER 3

PLANNING AN OFFENSIVE

"The military ideal is to force an
opposing army to submit without
battle."

1
Forcing submission without battle

Sun Tzu states:

In accordance with standard military doctrine, a state preserved intact is better than a state destroyed in war. An army preserved intact is better than an army destroyed in war. Battalions, companies and squads preserved intact are better than battalions, companies and squads destroyed in war.

Thus, winning a hundred victories in a hundred battles is not the military ideal. The military ideal is to force an opposing army to submit without battle.

2
Avoiding sieges

Striking against an opponent's plans is the most effective strategy. Striking at his alliances is the next most effective strategy. Striking at his military capabilities is next after that. Attacking his walled cities is the least effective strategy.

The rule is: attack walled cities only when there is no alternative. It takes upwards of three months to construct the wheeled screens, assault wagons and other weaponry and equipment needed for a siege. A further three months will pass while earth embankments are raised. Frustrated with the delay, a general may prematurely give the order to swarm the battlements, only to lose a third of his men in the assault and still not take the city. Such are the perils of siege warfare.

A great commander forces his opponents' armies to submit without battle. He captures their cities without having to attack them. He dismantles their states without protracted campaigns. He vies for supremacy throughout the world-under-heaven while keeping it intact.

So, he maximizes the military gains though his blades remain unblunted.

_____

3
Troop ratios for attack and retreat

Military doctrine teaches the following: with a ten-to-one advantage in troop numbers, encircle the enemy; when the ratio is five-to-one, launch an offensive; when double the enemy's size, split his forces; when evenly matched, be capable of giving battle; when outnumbered, be capable of mounting an effective defense; when clearly no match for the enemy, be capable of swiftly withdrawing.

An armed force strong enough to defy minor opponents, nevertheless falls prey to a major opponent.

_____

4
The general and the state

A good general is as a brace on the chariot of state. So long as that brace is sturdy, the state remains strong. If the brace cracks, the state is certain to weaken.

_____

5
Three types of interference by the sovereign

Now, a sovereign may sabotage his own army in three ways:

He orders the army to advance, not realizing that it is in no position to do so, or he orders it to withdraw, not realizing that it is in no position to do so. This inhibits the army's tactical autonomy.

He interferes with management of the Triple Corps,[2] despite being unversed in army affairs. This generates confusion among the officers.

He intervenes in senior appointments within the Triple Corps, without regard for existing lines of authority. This causes uncertainty among the officers.

Confusion and uncertainty within the Triple Corps attract trouble from foreign princes. In short, a disorderly army invites defeat.

_____

2   "Triple Corps" refers to the partition of the army into three divisions in the field (centre, left and right) or alternatively the coordination of three armies to achieve the same effect. In Sun Tzu it doubles as a general term for the army.

6
Five indicators of victory

Now, five indicators herald victory:

Recognizing when circumstances are ripe for battle and when they are not, heralds victory.

Understanding how to utilize troops in situations of both numerical superiority and numerical inferiority, heralds victory.

Sharing a common purpose up and down the line of command, heralds victory.

Taking full precautions against an adversary who is less well prepared, heralds victory.

Having a chief commander in charge of the campaign, unhampered by his sovereign, heralds victory.

These are the five indicators signifying that victory lies ahead.

7
Knowing conditions on both sides

Thus it is said:

When one understands the condition of the opposition and the condition of one's own side, one fights a hundred battles without ever facing defeat.

When one does not understand the condition of the opposition, but does understand the condition of one's own side, one loses one battle for every battle won.

When one understands neither the condition of the opposition nor the condition of one's own side, one faces defeat in every battle.

CHAPTER 4

DISPOSITION OF FORCES

"A winning force first secures victory,
then goes into battle."

1
Defense first

Sun Tzu states:

The best tacticians of old first made themselves invincible, then watched for their enemies to determine their own defeat.

Being invincible is something that one decides for oneself, but it is the enemy who determines his own defeat.

In other words, a great tactician may ensure his own side is invincible, but he cannot condemn the enemy to certain defeat.

Thus we say that victory can be known in advance, but it cannot be forced.

Being invincible depends on defense. Being able to beat the enemy depends on attack. One defends when one cannot counter the enemy's strength. One attacks when one's own strength is in surplus.

The best exponents of defense are unassailable, as if concealed in the depths of the earth. The best exponents of attack are unopposable, as if wielding the might of the entire heavens.

In this way, they preserve their own forces and secure complete victory.

2
Ease of victory

Forecasting a victory that everyone knows is coming, is not what distinguishes the greatest commanders. Receiving universal acclaim after winning a victory, is not what distinguishes the greatest commanders.

After all, lifting a strand of fur does not require unusual strength. Observing the sun and moon in the sky does not require sharp eyes. Hearing the sound of thunder does not require keen ears.

Those regarded as the best tacticians of old, overcame easy opponents.

The victories of the best tacticians earn them neither a reputation for wisdom nor accolades for courage. Their victories are so flawless as to be utterly one-sided, against foes who are already beaten.

A great tactician establishes an impregnable position, then defeats the enemy at the first opportunity.

So, a winning force first secures victory, then goes into battle. A losing force first goes into battle, then seeks victory.

A great commander cultivates his moral and political authority and champions institutional order. In this way, he alone is capable of determining the military outcome.

3
From measurements, to victory

Standard doctrine specifies five stages to victory:
~ First, initial measurements
~ Second, resource estimations
~ Third, numerical calculation
~ Fourth, comparative assessment
~ Fifth, victory.

From the ground one takes initial measurements. From measurements one estimates resources on both sides. On the basis of those estimates one calculates logistical requirements. The calculations allow one to assess comparative advantage, and from comparative advantage comes victory.

4
Overwhelming victory

So, the army that wins is like a one-pound weight on the scales, opposite a single grain. The army that loses is like a single grain on the scales, opposite a one-pound weight.

The troops of a victorious army surge into battle like a flash flood crashing through a mile-deep gorge.[3]

That concludes the topic of disposition of forces.

---

3   The text refers to a "thousand-*ren* gorge". A *ren* is equivalent to around 2 meters or a fathom.

CHAPTER 5

STRATEGIC DOMINANCE

"Battles generally begin with orthodox
openings, but it is the unconventional
move that wins the day."

1
Commanding a mass of troops

Sun Tzu states:

Organizing a mass of troops is the same as organizing a small detachment. It is a matter of segmenting them into units.

Commanding a mass of troops on the battlefield is the same as commanding a small detachment. It is a matter of formations and signalling.

The troops of the Triple Corps can be orchestrated to withstand any amount of enemy pressure without conceding. It is a matter of blending unconventional and orthodox tactics.

When troops take action, the impact must be that of a whetstone flung against an egg. It is a matter of asymmetrical force.

2
Tactical possibilities

Battles generally begin with orthodox openings, but it is the unconventional move that wins the day.

The options available to the best exponents of the unconventional are as boundless as heaven and earth. They spring without cease, like rivers and creeks.

Like the sun and the moon, which set then rise restored. Like the seasons, which pass then return renewed.

The pentatonic scale has only five notes, but combining

them generates more variations than could ever be listened to.

A painter's palette has only five colours, but combining them generates more variations than could ever be looked at.

Cookery uses only five basic flavours, but combining them generates more variations than could ever be sampled.

Strategic dominance is built on only two types of tactic, the unconventional and the orthodox, but combining them generates more variations than could ever be known.

Unconventional and orthodox tactics seed each other in an endless cycle. Who could ever exhaust the tactical possibilities?

3
Strategic dominance

Like a torrent, forceful enough to tumble boulders – that's strategic dominance.

Like a diving hawk, swift enough to break its prey on impact – that's striking at the decisive moment.

A great tactician combines fearsome strategic dominance with the capacity to strike at the decisive moment.

Gaining strategic dominance is like drawing taut a crossbow. Striking at the decisive moment is like releasing the trigger.

4
Managing chaos

Amid the tumult of battle, the fighting is chaotic but your forces do not descend into disorder. Amid the melee, your formations flex but they do not succumb.

Disorder on one side comes from order on the other. Faintheartedness on one side comes from courage on the other. Weakness on one side comes from strength on the other.

Segmentation of troops brings order to the disordered

Strategic dominance fills the fainthearted with courage.

Battle formations give strength to the weak.

A deft tactician maneuvers his opponents at will. He dictates formations and the enemy has to comply. He proffers bait and the enemy has to take it. He lures the enemy with the promise of gain, meanwhile poised with his elite units.

5
Logs and boulders

So, a great tactician seeks victory through strategic dominance, rather than looking to others to deliver victory for him. He selects the right men and works with them to achieve and exploit strategic dominance.

For the commander who successfully exploits strategic dominance, giving battle is akin to rolling logs and boulders down a slope.

By the nature of things, logs and boulders lie still when all is stable and tend towards motion on a steep slope. They stay put if they are angular but roll if rounded. The strategic dominance of a great campaigner is like the momentum of rounded boulders rolling down the flank of a mile-high mountain.

That concludes the topic of strategic dominance.

CHAPTER 6

DISPERSAL AND CONCENTRATION OF FORCES

"An accomplished campaigner imposes
his will on the opponent rather than
being imposed upon."

CHRISTOPHER MACDONALD

1
Imposing one's will

Sun Tzu states:

When an army arrives at the battleground first and waits for the enemy, its troops have time to recuperate. When an army arrives later and scrambles into position, its troops are worn-out before battle begins.

So, an accomplished campaigner imposes his will on the opponent rather than being imposed upon. He entices the enemy to move of his own accord into the intended position. He deters the enemy from going where he would otherwise go.

He can harass a rested enemy until that enemy is exhausted. He can make a well-provisioned enemy go hungry. He can make a settled enemy up sticks and move.

2
No discernible dispositions

Emerge where the enemy has no time to respond. Speed to wherever least anticipated.

March hundreds of miles without exhausting the troops, by keeping to areas where the enemy is absent.

Attack and be certain of seizing the objective, by striking where the enemy is undefended.

Defend and be sure of holding the position, by defending where the enemy will not attack.

So, against an accomplished attacker, the enemy does

163

not know where to defend. Against an accomplished defender, the enemy does not know where to attack.

Subtlety, such subtlety! An army with no discernible dispositions. Uncanny, so uncanny! Not a whisper betrays the army's movements. In this way you may put the enemy at your mercy.

3
Asymmetrical pressure

To advance without being repulsed, thrust where opposing forces are most dispersed. To withdraw without being pursued, move too swiftly for the opponent to react.

So, when we choose to do battle, the enemy has no choice but to engage with us, even though he is shielded behind battlements and ditches. Our attack is directed at a point he has to save.

And when we choose to avoid battle, there is nothing the enemy can do about it, though separated from us by no more than a line in the dirt. His forces are misdirected by our ploys.

4
Numerical advantage

Now, while we determine the dispositions of the opposing forces, our own dispositions cannot be discerned. This allows us to concentrate while the enemy remains dispersed. We converge as one while the enemy is spread across ten locations. It means we have overwhelming numerical superiority, attacking with a ten-to-one advantage. Our numerical superiority, going into battle, renders our adversary helpless.

The enemy cannot be certain where we have chosen to do battle. Since he cannot be certain, he has to be manned and equipped in several places at once. Since he is manned and equipped in several places, he is outnumbered wherever we choose to fight.

With his front line fully manned, he is depleted at the rear, and with his rear fully manned he is depleted at the front. With his left flank fully manned, he is depleted on the right, and with his right fully manned he is depleted on the left. When he is manned for battle at all points, then his forces are thin on the ground at all points.

Being outnumbered is the price one pays for preparing against every conceivable attack. Numerical superiority is what one gains by making the enemy prepare for every conceivable attack.

So, having determined in advance the place and time of battle, the army is perfectly set for battle even after marching hundreds of miles.

If the place and time of battle are uncertain, however, then the left flank cannot relieve the right flank and the right flank cannot relieve the left flank. The vanguard cannot relieve the rear guard and the rear guard cannot relieve the vanguard. The farthest-flung battalions may be dozens of miles apart, and even the closest are separated by a mile or more.

5
Neutralizing a stronger enemy

By my reckoning, even though Yue has more men at arms than we do, it will be of little benefit. In fact, I declare that victory is ours for the taking.

Despite an enemy's advantage in numbers, he can be neutralized as follows:

~ Analyse his strategy and understand his tactical priorities.

~ Prod him into action to study his patterns of movement.

~ Manipulate his dispositions to locate his critical vulnerabilities.

~ Skirmish to test where his forces are in surplus and where they are under-strength.

6
Mastery of dispositions

The ultimate in troop dispositions is to have no discernible dispositions. Since we have no discernible dispositions, the enemy's spies cannot detect our intentions and his strategists cannot counter-plan against us.

Mastery of dispositions enables us to steer the troops to victory, although they are not aware how it is done. Everyone knows of our dispositions at the moment of victory, but no one knows the dispositions by which we make victory possible in the first place.

So, victories are not replicable. They vary infinitely, according to dispositions on the day.

7
Fluidity and flexibility

Military dispositions should be as fluid as water. By its nature, water skirts high ground and flows downhill. By the same token, military forces bypass concentrations of troops and strike where the enemy is most dispersed.

Water forms channels according to the lie of the land, and armies fashion victory according to the presence of the enemy. Military action does not follow fixed strategic patterns any more than water keeps a constant shape.

Achieving victory while accommodating the enemy's transformations along the way, is the mark of military genius.

None of the five natural elements permanently prevails. None of the four seasons permanently endures. The days shorten, then lengthen again. The moon both wanes and waxes.

CHAPTER 7

MANEUVERING FOR ADVANTAGE

"By side-tracking the opponent and
distracting him with easy gains, one
reaches the battlefield first despite
marching later."

1
Misdirection

Sun Tzu states:

In accordance with standard military doctrine, the commander-in-chief is mandated by the sovereign to raise an army and rally the troops for war. He assembles the various contingents and provides for them to be encamped.

The hardest part is maneuvering for advantage over the opposing army. The challenge is to advance directly by circuitous means, turning adversity to advantage along the way.

For example, by side-tracking the opponent and distracting him with easy gains, one reaches the battlefield first despite marching later. This is a matter of mastering the interplay between oblique and direct maneuvers.

2
Opportunities and risks

Now, pre-battle maneuvers create opportunities, and they create risks.

For example, a fully equipped column sent to exploit an immediate opportunity, arrives too late. On the other hand, a light force despatched for the same purpose, must take to the field without its full complement of weapons and equipment.

When the men are ordered to bundle their armour and race

30 miles[4] to exploit an opportunity, marching double
distances without stopping for the night, it ends with
the capture of the entire corps and its commanders. The
more dynamic units arrive first, while those that are
slacker bring up the rear. In the event, only one in ten of
the troops reach the field in time for battle.
A rapid march of 15 miles ends with the vanguard being
repulsed and its commanders seized. Around half of
those who set out, arrive to schedule.
A rapid march of 10 miles results in around two-thirds of
the troops arriving to schedule.
An army without heavy weaponry and equipment is
doomed. An army without provisions is doomed. An
army without reserve supplies is doomed.

3
Principles of maneuvering for advantage

Now, one cannot enter into an alliance with a foreign prince
without first knowing his objectives. By the same token,
one cannot begin a march until one is familiar with the
features of the terrain – the wooded mountains, canyons
and crags, marshes and bogs. Moreover, one cannot
exploit the natural advantages of the terrain without
support from local guides.
Now, military forces establish decoy positions to fool the

---

4   The distances cited in this section are 100 *li*, 50 *li* and 30 *li*, converted here to
     30 miles, 15 miles and 10 miles respectively. A *li* is equivalent to about a third
     of a mile.

enemy, move when there is advantage to be gained, and divide and merge for tactical variation.

So, the army must be as fleet as the wind, but rooted like a forest. It must raid like wildfire, but be as unmoveable as a mountain. It must be as impenetrable as the dark, yet strike like lightning.

When plundering the countryside, assign each unit its own district. When annexing new territory, parcel out the gains.

Weigh up the strategic benefits before making a move.

The commander who best masters the interplay between oblique and direct maneuvers, will prevail.

These are the principles of maneuvering for advantage.

4
Signalling

The treatise *Army Management* states:

"Instructions and responses are not always audible in battle, hence gongs and drums. Visual cues cannot always be seen, hence banners and pennants."

Gongs, drums, banners and pennants are used to unify the ears and eyes of the troops.

With everyone's attention thus focussed, the courageous do not advance without backup and the fainthearted do not withdraw without orders. This applies for any mass of soldiers.

So, night fighting is signalled for the most part by torch and drum, and daytime battle is signalled for the most part

using banners and pennants. This is how to commandeer
the ears and eyes of the men.

5
Gaining the upper hand

The troops of the entire Triple Corps may become
   demoralized. Their generals may lose heart.
Likening the campaign to a single day, we may say that
   morale peaks in the morning then declines as the day
   wears on. By evening, the men are homesick.
An expert commander avoids battle when the opponent's
   morale is at its peak, and strikes instead when enemy
   troops are tired and homesick. In terms of morale, his
   side gains the upper hand.
He holds formation and watches for disorder on the other
   side, monitoring in silence as the din rises. In terms of
   mental discipline, his side gains the upper hand.
He takes up position close to the battleground and waits
   for the enemy to arrive from afar. With troops who are
   rested and fed, he awaits an opponent who is weary and
   hungry. In terms of physical condition, his side gains the
   upper hand.
He neither engages an opponent whose banners are
   impeccably aligned, nor attacks an opponent whose
   dispositions form an imposing array. In terms of tactical
   flexibility, his side gains the upper hand.

6
Maneuvering in proximity to the enemy

In accordance with military doctrine, always observe the following:
~ Do not advance uphill towards the enemy.
~ Do not oppose an enemy descending from high ground.
~ Do not pursue an enemy pretending to flee.
~ Do not attack the enemy's elite units.
~ Do not be baited by vulnerable enemy units.
~ Do not obstruct a homebound army.
~ Do leave a gap for an army that you have surrounded.
~ Do not press a desperate foe too hard.
These are part of standard military doctrine.

CHAPTER 8

NINE SCENARIOS REQUIRING TACTICAL FLEXIBILITY

"The wise commander prudently factors
in a range of circumstances,
both favourable and
otherwise."

1
Mobilization

Sun Tzu states:

In accordance with standard military doctrine, the commander-in-chief is mandated by the sovereign to raise an army and rally the troops for war.

_____

2
Cautionary precepts

~ Do not make camp in an adverse-terrain zone[5]

~ Do form alliances in a junction zone

~ Do not linger in a cut-off zone

~ Do be ready with stratagems in an encirclement zone, and

~ Do give battle when caught in a fight-to-the-death zone.

Furthermore, there exist:

~ routes which should not be marched

~ armies which should not be attacked

~ walled cities which should not be stormed, and

~ tracts of territory which should not be contested.

By the same token, there are orders from the sovereign which may be disregarded.

_____

---

5   These five categories, from **adverse-terrain zone** to **fight-to-the-death zone**, are described in Ch. 11, passage 1.

3
Tactical flexibility

A general who is expert in the tactical flexibility needed for the nine scenarios above, knows how to employ force to best effect. A general who lacks that expertise, cannot turn terrain to advantage even when he knows all about the terrain and its features.

A commander who lacks the tactical flexibility required for the nine scenarios above, will never realize the potential of his troops, even though he knows of the advantages connected with the five zonal scenarios.

The wise commander prudently factors in a range of circumstances, both favourable and otherwise. He inspires confidence in his approach by pursuing advantage, and he averts peril by preparing for setbacks.

4
Never rely on the opponent

So, pressure foreign princes with threats, harry them with undertakings and busy them with incentives.

In accordance with military doctrine, never rely on the opponent opting not to advance, only on one's own capacity to respond when he does. Never rely on the opponent opting not strike, only on one's own position being unassailable.

5
Five fatal traits in a general

Now, generals are prone to five fatal traits.
~ If reckless, a general gets himself killed
~ If survival is his priority, he gets captured
~ If hot-tempered, he is easily provoked
~ If he is fastidious about honor, he can be shamed
~ If he cares too much about his men, he can be distracted.
The general is at fault in each of these five scenarios, with calamitous consequences for the campaign. Whenever an army is routed and its commanders killed, it invariably involves one of these five traits.
It is imperative that this be studied and understood in depth.

CHAPTER 9

ARMIES ON THE MARCH

"While we keep hazardous terrain in
front of us, the enemy has it to
his rear."

1
Positioning the army

Sun Tzu states:

The following principles apply when establishing a position in proximity to the enemy:

Keep to the valleys when traversing mountain country. Occupy elevated ground with a southerly prospect. Do not march uphill into battle. This is how to establish a position in mountain country.

When crossing a river, attain the opposite bank then move clear. If the opponent crosses towards you, do not confront him mid-channel. Attack once half his force has come across. This is a good opportunity. When you need to initiate battle, never do so alongside a body of water. Occupy elevated ground with a southerly prospect, and do not face upstream. This is how to establish a position close to water.

When crossing marshland, proceed rapidly and do not linger. If you have to engage the enemy among marshes, then keep to firmer, grassy ground with woods to your rear. This is how to establish a position in marshland.

On level terrain, occupy a readily accessible position with elevated ground to the right and rear. Keep the fight-to-the-death zone in front and safety behind you. This is how to establish a position on level terrain.

In each of the four scenarios above, the army profits from establishing the right position. These principles enabled the Yellow Emperor to defeat his four main rivals.

Armies seek out elevated, bright positions and shun those that are low-lying and sunless. They occupy firm ground in salutary surroundings, ensuring low rates of sickness.

This is the mark of a victorious army.

On hillsides and embankments you must take up position on the sunward side with the slope to your right and rear.

This is how to gain military advantage from the lay of the land.

2
Hazardous terrain

When it rains upstream and the river begins to churn, wait for the water to subside before attempting to ford.

When the terrain includes ravines, sinkholes, deep hollows, thick brush, bogs or crevasses, it is important to move rapidly away and stay away. While we keep our distance from such terrain, the enemy moves onto it. While we keep hazardous terrain in front of us, the enemy has it to his rear.

It is essential to reconnoitre if your route passes among gullies, crags, swamps, natural basins, reed meadows, wooded mountains or areas of dense undergrowth. These are classic locations for ambush and surveillance.

3
Situations to be wary of

When the enemy is nearby and remains motionless, it means he has found terrain that is to his advantage. When he tries to provoke battle from a distance, he wants you to advance. If his position invites attack, it is a ruse.

If you see mass movement of trees, it means the enemy is approaching. Where there is tall grass and plenty of natural screens, you must be wary.

Where birds rise suddenly into the air, it tells you men are hidden there. When wild creatures are spooked, a sudden attack is imminent.

A high column of dust ahead indicates that chariots are approaching, whereas a low plume of dust means that infantry is on its way. Scattered streaks of dust show that troops are gathering firewood, while wisps of dust here and there mean that the enemy is making camp.

Conciliatory words accompanied by intensified preparations indicate that the enemy is getting ready to advance. Verbal bluster accompanied by aggressive moves means that the enemy is going to withdraw.

When light chariots fan out on the wings, the enemy is shaping up for battle.

When the enemy requests a truce out of the blue, it is a ploy. When his men rush to take up position, the attack is imminent. When his army seems to part-advance and part-retreat, the intention is to lure you forward.

4
Signs the enemy is in difficulty

When enemy soldiers can be seen propped on their weapons, it is a sign of hunger. When the water carriers drink first, the troops are parched.

When the enemy fails to advance to capitalize on an opportunity, it means his forces are fatigued.

When birds flock to the enemy encampment, it means it is deserted.

When enemy soldiers cry out at night, it means they are terrified.

When there is commotion in the enemy ranks, it means the men have lost respect for their commanders. When their banners can be seen milling around at random, discipline has broken down. When the officers rant and rave, it means they can no longer rouse the men.

When enemy troops slay their horses for meat, then leave their cooking pots scattered on the ground and do not return to camp, it means they will fight like men with nothing to lose.

When enemy soldiers cluster in groups, whispering and muttering, it means that their high command has lost control. When rewards are promised to all and sundry, it is a mark of desperation. When punishment is rife, it shows that the situation is dire. When officers alternately harangue then plead with the men, it betrays their utter ineptness.

When the enemy seeks to parley, he wants a break in hostilities.

When the enemy aggressively confronts us and locks into position, neither initiating battle nor withdrawing, then the situation calls for careful analysis.

5
Confronting a larger force

In armed conflict, the number of men on either side is not what matters most. When confronted by a more numerous foe, simply avoid launching a frontal assault. Instead, concentrate your forces, anticipate the enemy's movements and rally morale.

A commander who does not plan for such contingencies and underestimates the enemy, inevitably gets captured.

6
Loyalty and discipline

Soldiers subjected to harsh punishments before they have learned to be loyal, incline to insubordination. This kind is difficult to command. Soldiers who are already loyal but know that punishments will not be carried out, cannot be commanded at all.

So, issue orders in accordance with civil norms, but enforce discipline by martial means. This guarantees the men's allegiance.

Orders must be executed consistently as an example to all, to ensure obedience. If a precedent is set that orders are not executed consistently, then the men learn to disobey.

When orders are executed consistently, a commander can depend on his men and the men can depend on their commander.

CHAPTER 10

TERRAIN

"Going to war fully aware of the
principles of terrain,
ensures victory."

1
Six types of terrain

Sun Tzu states:

These are the main types of terrain: "accessible", "hanging", "branch", "constricted", "craggy" and "remote".

Terrain that is equally open to advance by either us or the enemy, is considered accessible. The first to arrive on accessible terrain occupies high ground on the sunward side with good supply lines. That army has the advantage in battle.

Terrain which allows for easy progress in one direction but not the other is described as hanging. On hanging terrain we may advance swiftly and defeat the enemy provided he is unprepared. If the enemy is prepared, however, and we fail to defeat him, then it will be difficult to withdraw. This is a situation to avoid.

Terrain on which neither side gains the advantage by emerging first, is described as branch terrain. If the enemy tries to lure us onto branch terrain, we do not respond. Instead we back off, drawing the enemy out then striking once he is half exposed. This is a good opportunity.

On constricted terrain, if we arrive first, we take up a blocking position and await the enemy. If the enemy is there first, we hold back if he has occupied a blocking position and advance if not.

On craggy terrain, if we arrive first, we occupy high ground on the sunward side and await the enemy. If the enemy is there first, we back off and draw him into the open. We do not advance.

On remote terrain, where the warring parties are evenly

matched, it is difficult to initiate battle and there is nothing to be gained by doing so.

These are the principles for exploiting the six types of terrain. Understanding this is among the most important duties of a general. It is imperative that this be studied and understood in depth.

——————————

2
How armies fail in battle

Now, military action may fail in one of the following ways:
~ soldiers flee the fighting
~ discipline collapses
~ units cave in
~ formations break up
~ the army disintegrates in chaos
~ the army is routed.

None of these six calamities can be blamed on natural conditions. It is the general who is at fault in each case.

When, all else being equal, one army takes on another ten times its size, the result is that soldiers flee the fighting.

When an army has tough troops but feeble officers, there will be a collapse in discipline.

When an army has tough officers but feeble troops, then units cave in under pressure.

When flag officers, agitated in the presence of the enemy and inclined to disregard orders, trigger the attack before their high command has full measure of the situation, then formations break up.

When generals are weak and the troops neither fear nor respect them, when the disciplinary code is unclear, when key personnel are continually shuffled around and when dispositions are in disarray, then the outcome is that the army disintegrates in chaos.

When generals fail to read the situation correctly and, for example, pitch a small contingent against a massed enemy, or use a weak unit to strike a strong opponent, or advance into battle without a vanguard, then the outcome is a rout.

These are the six routes to defeat. Understanding them is among the most important duties of a general. It is imperative that this be studied and understood in depth.

3
Understanding terrain

Terrain is essential to the success of any military operation. The best generals assess the challenges of the terrain and plan for the distances involved, so as to anticipate the enemy and create conditions for victory.

Going to war fully aware of the principles of terrain, ensures victory. Going to war ignorant of those principles, ensures defeat.

4
Qualities in a commander

Now, when the prospect of victory is assured, it is right to do battle even if the sovereign has stated that there should be no battle. By the same token it is right to avoid battle when defeat is certain, even if the sovereign has stated that battle is necessary.

The commander who neither seeks glory by advancing nor shirks responsibility for retreating, whose sole concern is the security of the nation and whose objectives accord with those of his sovereign, is an invaluable asset to any state.

When a commander is as concerned for his men's safety as if they were infants, they will venture with him into the deepest gorge. When he values their lives as if they were his own sons, they will battle to the death alongside him.

On the other hand, if a commander is indulgent and lacks authority, if he cossets the men and fails to enforce orders, if he tolerates indiscipline and does not impose control, then the army becomes as intractable as a spoiled child.

5
Understanding conditions on both sides

If we know only that our troops are ready to attack but not whether the enemy is vulnerable to attack, then we can only be half certain of victory.

If we know only that the enemy is vulnerable to attack but

not whether our troops are ready to attack, then we can only be half certain of victory.

If we know both that the enemy is vulnerable to attack and that our troops are ready to attack, but are unaware that the terrain does not favour battle, then we can still only be half certain of victory.

So, a seasoned commander is never disoriented when he makes his move. He always has options in reserve when he takes action.

Thus it is said that when a commander understands equally well the condition of the opposition and the condition of his own side, his victory is never in doubt. When a commander understands equally well the prevailing conditions and the terrain for the campaign, then victory is secure.

CHAPTER 11

NINE TYPES OF CAMPAIGN ZONE

"The general rule for an invasion force
is that the deeper it penetrates,
the more compact
it becomes."

1
The nine campaign zones

Sun Tzu states:

In accordance with military doctrine, there are nine types of
campaign zone: dispersion zones, light-incursion zones,
contestable zones, encounter zones, junction zones,
heavy-invasion zones, adverse-terrain zones, enclosed
zones and fight-to-the-death zones.

When a prince gives battle on home territory, then his army
is in a dispersion zone.[6]

Crossing a small way into enemy territory puts the army in
a light-incursion zone.

An area considered equally advantageous to both ourselves
and our opponents, is considered a contestable zone.

An area equally accessible to ourselves and our opponents,
is an encounter zone.

The first army to claim an area where the approaches to
three principalities intersect, stands to dominate in
every direction. This is described as a junction zone.

When an army penetrates deep into enemy territory, with
walled cities to its rear, it is in a heavy-invasion zone.

Any area where progress is made difficult by features of
the terrain such as wooded mountains, canyons and
crags, and marshes and bogs, is described as an adverse-
terrain zone.

An area reached by a narrow approach with no direct line
of retreat, rendering the army vulnerable to attack by a
far smaller force, is an enclosed zone.

When immediate battle offers the only lifeline, while delay

---

6   This is where troops are prone to desert for their villages.

means certain annihilation, then the army is in the fight-to-the-death zone.

In sum, do not give battle in a dispersion zone, do not linger in a light-incursion zone, do not attack in a contestable zone, do not attempt to strand the enemy in an encounter zone, do form alliances in a junction zone, do plunder provisions in a heavy-invasion zone, do press ahead in an adverse-terrain zone, do adapt stratagems for an enclosed zone and do give battle in the fight-to-the-death zone.

2
Manipulating the enemy

The great commanders of antiquity would manipulate an enemy force such that its forward units were isolated from those further back, that the main body of the army and its smaller detachments were out of step, that elite and regular troops were unable to relieve one another, that the flow of information up and down the line of command was blocked, and that the infantry were either spread too far apart to act in concert or were unevenly bunched together.

Move only when it suits your purpose. Otherwise stay put.

The question is: how to handle an enemy who is readying to attack with a large, well-marshalled force?

My answer: take the initiative and seize something precious to him. Now he will be at your bidding.

In war, speed is of the essence. Aim to catch the enemy off

guard. Emerge from the direction you are least expected
and attack where he is least prepared.

3
Deep invasion

The general rule for an invasion force is that the deeper it
penetrates the more compact it becomes, to the point
where it can no longer be outfought. The Triple Corps
armies plunder farmland as they go so as to secure the
provisions they need.
Be attentive to the physical condition of the troops and do
not exhaust them. Conserve strength and build morale.
Keep the opposition guessing as to your movements
and your plans.
When soldiers are cornered, they fight to the death rather
than trying to flee. Faced with death, officers and men
alike give every ounce of their strength. How could it
be otherwise?
Extreme situations make soldiers fearless. When there
is nowhere to run, they stand firm. Being deep inside
enemy territory solidifies the army. The men fight
because there is no alternative.
An army in such circumstances is sharp and alert, regardless
of training. The men do whatever needs to be done
without being told. They are loyal without swearing
oaths of allegiance. They can be depended on, with or
without orders.
Ban superstitious practices and quash doubts. Free of such

distractions, the men will fight to the bitter end.

Our officers are not rich, but that is not because they disdain material wealth. Their days may be numbered, but that does not mean they disdain long life.

When they hear the order to deploy for battle, the men and their officers are so afraid that tears wet the tunics of those who are sitting up and stain the cheeks of those lying down. Yet when cornered, with nowhere to run, those same men are as brave as any Zhuan Zhu or Cao Gui.[7]

4
Uniting the army

A well-commanded army is like the snake known as the "quick-as-a-flash", which lives in the Heng Mountains. Strike its head and it lashes back with its tail. Strike the tail and it lashes back with its head. Strike in the middle and it lashes back with both head and tail.

The question is: can an army be trained to respond as reflexively as the "quick-as-a-flash"? The answer: yes, it can.

The peoples of Wu and Yue detest each other, but when a mixed group of them is in a boat that gets struck by a squall mid-channel, they pull together like a pair of hands.

Simply hobbling the horses and embedding the chariot

---

7   Two celebrated do-or-die assassins from antiquity.

wheels in the ground does not guarantee that the men
will stay and fight.

When a military operation is well-managed, it is possible
to attain consistent levels of courage throughout the
army. When terrain is properly exploited, it is possible to
obtain maximum commitment from all units, whether
battle-hardened or not.

So, a great commander directs his troops as if guiding a
single person by the hand. They follow without a qualm.

5
The role of a commander

It is the business of the chief commander to keep his own
counsel, and manage army affairs in a manner that is
just and proper.

He keeps officers and men in the dark about his intentions,
so that no-one other than himself sees the full picture.

He switches tack and revises plans such that he can never
be second-guessed.

He overnights at various locations and travels by diverse
routes so that no one can be sure where he will turn up
next.

When he brings the army to the brink of battle, it is as if a
ladder back to the ground has been kicked away.

He inserts the army deep into foreign territory, and only
then releases the trigger.

He has the boats burned and cauldrons smashed. He herds
the army in one direction then another, like a flock of

THE SCIENCE OF WAR

sheep, until the men have no idea where they are.

He masses the troops of the Triple Corps and delivers them into the teeth of danger. Such is the role of the chief commander.

The tactical variations associated with the nine types of campaign zone, the benefits of extending and contracting one's forces, the mood and morale of men at arms – it is imperative that each of these matters is studied and understood in depth.

6
Campaign-zone priorities

The general rule for an invasion force is that the deeper it penetrates, the more compact it becomes. Invade only a little way and the troops are prone to desert.

Once an army leaves its homeland and crosses into enemy territory, it enters a cut-off zone.

An area accessible from several directions, is a junction zone.

Pressing deep into enemy territory puts an army into a heavy-invasion zone.

Crossing a small way into enemy territory puts the army in a light-incursion zone.

When retreat is blocked and the way ahead is narrow, then the army is in an enclosed zone.

When there is no way out, the army is in a fight-to-the-death zone.

In the dispersion zone our generals infuse the troops with

common resolve. In the light-incursion zone our generals keep their divisions grouped together. In the contestable zone our generals quicken the pace of the rear guard. In the encounter zone our generals pay particular attention to defense. In the junction zone our generals consolidate alliances. In the heavy-invasion zone our generals secure the supply of provisions. In the adverse-terrain zone our generals press ahead. In the enclosed zone our generals ensure that openings in the perimeter are plugged. And in the fight-to-the-death zone our generals demonstrate readiness to give their lives in battle.

In war, it is natural to resist when surrounded, to fight when there is no alternative and, in circumstances of extreme danger, to obey any order that is given.

7
Understand the terrain

Now, one cannot enter into an alliance with a foreign prince without first knowing his objectives. By the same token, one cannot begin a march until one is familiar with the features of the terrain – the wooded mountains, canyons and crags, marshes and bogs. Moreover, one cannot exploit the natural advantages of the terrain without support from local guides.

8
Overawe the enemy

Those who command the armies of a mighty king cannot afford to be ignorant of any of these various points.

When a mighty king launches a military strike against another powerful state, the state he attacks does not even manage to mobilize in its own defense. The attacker overawes with such authority that the enemy can gather no allies in its support.

A kingdom that dominates to that degree does not have to jockey for alliances or nurture proxies far and wide. Being confident in its own designs and having the authority to overawe any enemy, it can pick off foreign cities and crush rival states at will.

9
Motivation

Offer rewards that go beyond standard practice, and issue commands without ceremony. Maneuver the massed men of the Triple Corps as if guiding a single person.

Give instructions for the mission without explaining your intentions. Motivate the men with opportunity rather than stressing the dangers involved.

Place soldiers in a doomed position, and they will survive. Trap them in the fight-to-the-death zone, and they will stay alive.

A body of troops facing disaster can yet fashion victory out of the situation.

10
Scrutinize the enemy's intentions

The business of warfare entails scrutinizing the enemy's intentions. Shadow the enemy for hundreds of miles before eliminating his high command. This is known as accomplishing the mission by cunning and ability.

11
Act quickly

On the day you announce mobilization, close the passes and break the bamboo tallies used at border crossings. Prevent enemy envoys from entering the country.

Convene in the confines of the national altar-hall to carry out the necessary planning.

Quickly exploit gaps in the enemy's defenses. Begin by seizing something that is precious to him. Subtly schedule the timing of the main battle.

Manage the course of battle by adapting to the enemy's approach rather than relying on pre-determined tactics.

At the outset, be as coy as a maiden. Wait until the enemy's door is ajar then make your move, swift as a darting hare. Caught unawares, the enemy will be powerless to resist.

CHAPTER 12

INCENDIARY ATTACKS

"When making an incendiary attack,
be sure to be ready for
various developments..."

1
Five types of incendiary attack

Sun Tzu states:

There are five types of incendiary attack:

~ First, incendiary attacks against soldiers

~ Second, incendiary attacks on stocks of provisions

~ Third, incendiary attacks on wagons and equipment

~ Fourth, incendiary attacks on the armoury

~ Fifth, incendiary attacks on supply lines

Incendiaries are needed for any attack by fire. Supplies of appropriate materials must be kept available.

2
How to attack using incendiaries

When starting a blaze, consider the season and select a suitable day. The best time of year is when the weather is hot and dry. Pick a day when the moon is in one of four constellations that herald windy conditions, namely the Winnowing Basket, the Wall, the Wings and the Chariot Board.

When making an incendiary attack, be sure to be ready for various developments associated with each type of attack. For example:

When a blaze breaks out inside the enemy camp, be ready to respond promptly from outside.

When a blaze breaks out but the enemy remains calm, wait and watch – do not attack. If practical, follow through as the flames peak. Otherwise, stay put.

Fires can be started outside the enemy perimeter, in which case do not wait for the flames to spread inside before making a move. Decide how and when to set fires according to the season.

When a fire is started upwind, do not attack from downwind. A wind that blows throughout the day will die down at night.

All armies need to know about launching and following through on the five types of incendiary attack, and must be logistically prepared to defend against such attacks.

Using fire as part of an offensive is a wise move. Flooding the enemy is also a powerful approach. However, while water may strand an opponent, it does not deprive that opponent of equipment and supplies in the same way that fire does.

3
Consolidate gains

Failing to consolidate the gains of battle is a deadly mistake. It is described as squandering valuable resources.

Thus it is said that while the clear-sighted ruler deliberates, the high-calibre general consolidates.

Do not move unless it is to your advantage. Do not deploy troops unless it brings gains. Do not give battle unless the situation is critical.

4
Prudence and vigilance

A ruler should never mobilize for war in a fit of rage. A general should never attack in anger.

Move only when it serves your purpose. Otherwise stay put.

Someone who is enraged, will laugh again. Someone who is angry, will be cheerful again. However, conquered kingdoms cannot be restored and dead men cannot be brought back to life.

So, the clear-sighted sovereign plans prudently for conflict, while the high-calibre general stays alert for danger.

In this way the nation is kept secure and its armies remain intact.

CHAPTER 13

INTELLIGENCE OPERATIONS

"There is no aspect of armed conflict
in which intelligence operations
do not play a part."

CHRISTOPHER MACDONALD

1
Knowing the enemy's intentions

Sun Tzu states:

Funding a 100,000-man army on a campaign hundreds of miles from home costs a thousand gold pieces per day. This is paid for by taxing the common people and exacting tribute from the nobility. In the ensuing upheaval at home and abroad, up to 700,000 households lose their means of livelihood, while the highways fill with people on the move.

A military standoff may persist for years before ending in a single day of combat.

Any commander who would forgo vital intelligence on the enemy simply to avoid disbursing honours and emoluments and a few hundred pieces of gold, is the epitome of inhumanity. He is no general to his men, no aide to his ruler, and no master of victory.

The reason that a clear-sighted sovereign and worthy general can together win every military encounter and establish a peerless record of success, is that they know the enemy's intentions in advance.

Advance knowledge is not obtained by appealing to spirits and gods. It cannot be deduced from known facts or calculated by astrological divination. It has to be obtained from people – people with information about the enemy.

2
Five types of intelligence source

Intelligence operations depend on five types of intelligence source: local informers, insiders, converts, dummy spies and active spies.

The web of connections that forms when all five types of intelligence source are in play, without others knowing about it, is considered "otherworldly." This is an invaluable asset for the sovereign.

Local informers are natives of enemy territory who supply us with intelligence.

Insiders are enemy officials who supply us with intelligence.

Converts are enemy spies and envoys who switch sides and supply us with intelligence.

Dummy spies are expendable agents on our side, deliberately fed misinformation to pass to the enemy.

Active spies are agents in the field who are called in to report their findings.

3
Managing intelligence operations

Among all the affairs of the Triple Corps, nothing is of more immediate concern to the chief commander than intelligence work. No one is more richly rewarded than spies, and no activity is more confidential than that of spies.

One cannot manage an intelligence network without

exceptionally good judgement. One cannot deploy intelligence assets without being humane and principled. One cannot obtain reliable intelligence without great subtlety and discretion.

Subtlety – it takes such subtlety! There is no aspect of armed conflict in which intelligence operations do not play a part. Should information about an intelligence operation be leaked in advance, then the agents concerned and anyone they spoke with must be executed.

4
The importance of converts

Whenever the army is preparing an attack, or there is a city to be stormed or a target to be assassinated, the first priority is to establish the identities of the generals on the other side, along with those of their lieutenants, aides-de-camp, sentries and personal retainers. We instruct our agents to obtain this information.

We make sure to identify enemy agents among us, then we induce them, with bribes and official residences, to switch allegiance. This is how we recruit converts.

Thanks to information obtained from converts, we are able to make use of local informers and enemy insiders. Thanks to information obtained from converts, we are able to feed misinformation to the enemy via dummy spies. Thanks to information obtained from converts, we are able to utilize our active spies at the right time.

The ruler must be aware of everything that happens

involving the five types of intelligence source, and he depends on converts for that awareness. It is therefore imperative that converts be lavishly rewarded.

Two examples from history:

~ The Yin dynasty succeeded the Xia dynasty thanks to Yi Zhi, originally a minister under the Xia.

~ The Zhou dynasty succeeded the Yin dynasty with help from Lu Ya, who had formerly served under the Yin.

5
Assured success

So, only the clear-sighted sovereign and worthy general can attract people of the highest calibre to provide intelligence. Success is thereby assured.

This is the essence of war. Every action of the Triple Corps hinges on it.

孫子兵法

THE SUN-TZU IN CHINESE

始計第一

1 孫子曰

　　兵者國之大事死生之地存亡之道

　　不可不察也

2 故經之以五事校之以計而索其情

　　　一曰道二曰天三曰地四曰將五曰法

　　　道者令民與上同意也故可與之死可與之生而不畏危

　　　天者陰陽寒暑時制也

　　　地者遠近險易廣狹死生也

　　　將者智信仁勇嚴也

　　　法者曲制官道主用也

　　　凡此五者將莫不聞知之者勝不知者不勝

　　　故校之以計而索其情

3 曰主孰有道將孰有能天地孰得法令孰行兵眾孰強士卒孰練賞罰孰明

　　　吾以此知勝負矣

4 將聽吾計用之必勝留之

　　　將不聽吾計用之必敗去之

　　　計利以聽乃為之勢以佐其外

　　　勢者因利而制權也

5 兵者詭道也

　　　故能而示之不能用而示之不用

近而示之遠遠而示之近

利而誘之亂而取之

實而備之強而避之

怒而撓之卑而驕之

佚而勞之親而離之

攻其無備出其不意

此兵家之勝不可先傳也

6 夫未戰而廟算勝者得算多也未戰而廟算不勝者得算少也

多算勝少算不勝而況於無算乎

吾以此觀之勝負見矣

作戰第二

1 孫子曰

凡用兵之法馳車千駟革車千乘帶甲十萬千裏饋糧

則內外之費賓客之用膠漆之材車甲之奉日費千金然後十萬之師舉矣

2 其用戰也貴勝久則鈍兵挫銳攻城則力屈久暴師則國用不足

夫鈍兵挫銳屈力殫貨則諸侯乘其弊而起雖有智者不能善其後矣

故兵聞拙速未睹巧之久也夫兵久而國利者未之有也

故不盡知用兵之害者則不能盡知用兵之利也

3 善用兵者役不再籍糧不三載

取用于國因糧于敵故軍食可足也國之貧于師者遠輸遠輸則百

姓貧

近于師者貴賣貴賣則百姓財竭財竭則急于丘没力屈財彈中原內虛于家

百姓之費十去其七公家之費破車罷馬甲冑矢弩戟楯蔽櫓丘牛大車十去其六

故智將務食於敵食敵一鐘當吾二十鐘秆一石當我二十石

4 故殺敵者怒也取敵之利者貨也

故車戰得車十乘已上賞其先得者而更其旌旗車雜而乘之卒善而養之是謂勝敵而益強

5 故兵貴勝不貴久

故知兵之將民之司命國家安危之主也

———————〰———————

謀攻第三

1 孫子曰

凡用兵之法全國爲上破國次之全軍爲上破軍次之全旅爲上破旅次之全卒爲上破卒次之全伍爲上破伍次之

是故百戰百勝非善之善者也不戰而屈人之兵善之善者也

2 故上兵伐謀其次伐交其次伐兵其下攻城

攻城之法爲不得已修櫓轒轀具器械三月而後成距闉又三月而後已將不勝其忿而蟻附之殺士卒三分之一而城不拔者此攻之災也

故善用兵者屈人之兵而非戰也拔人之城而非攻也毀人之國而非久也必以全爭于天下

故兵不頓而利可全此謀攻之法也

3 故用兵之法十則圍之五則攻之倍則分之敵則能戰之少則能守之不若則能避之

212

故小敵之堅大敵之擒也

4 夫將者國之輔也輔周則國必強輔隙則國必弱

5 故軍之所以患于君者三

不知軍之不可以進而謂之進不知軍之不可以退而謂之退是謂
縻軍

不知三軍之事而同三軍之政則軍士惑矣

不知三軍之權而同三軍之任則軍士疑矣

三軍既惑且疑則諸侯之難至矣是謂亂軍引勝

6 故知勝有五

知可以戰與不可以戰者勝

識衆寡之用者勝

上下同欲者勝

以虞待不虞者勝

將能而君不御者勝

此五者知勝之道也

7 故曰

知彼知己百戰不殆

不知彼而知己一勝一負

不知彼不知己每戰必敗

軍形第四

1 孫子曰

昔之善戰者先爲不可勝以待敵之可勝

不可勝在己可勝在敵

故善戰者能爲不可勝不能使敵必可勝

故曰勝可知而不可爲

不可勝者守也可勝者攻也守則不足攻則有餘

善守者藏于九地之下善攻者動于九天之上

故能自保而全勝也

2 見勝不過衆人之所知非善之善者也戰勝而天下曰善非善之善者也

故擧秋毫不爲多力見日月不爲明目聞雷霆不爲聰耳

古之所爲善戰者勝于易勝者

故善戰者之勝也無智名無勇功故其戰勝不忒不忒者其措必勝勝已敗者也

故善戰者立于不敗之地而不失敵之敗也

是故勝兵先勝而後求戰敗兵先戰而後求勝

善用兵者修道而保法故能爲勝敗之政

3 兵法一曰度二曰量三曰數四曰稱五曰勝

地生度度生量量生數數生稱稱生勝

4 故勝兵若以鎰稱銖敗兵若以銖稱鎰

勝者之戰民也若決積水于千仞之谿

形也

兵勢第五

1 孫子曰

　凡治衆如治寡分數是也

　鬥衆如鬥寡形名是也

　三軍之衆可使必受敵而無敗者奇正是也

　兵之所加如以碫投卵者虛實是也

2 凡戰者以正合以奇勝

　故善出奇者無窮如天地不竭如江河

　終而復始日月是也死而復生四時是也

　聲不過五五聲之變不可勝聽也

　色不過五五色之變不可勝觀也

　味不過五五味之變不可勝嘗也

　戰勢不過奇正奇正之變不可勝窮也

　奇正相生如循環之無端孰能窮之哉

3 激水之疾至于漂石者勢也

　鷙鳥之擊至于毀折者節也

　是故善戰者其勢險其節短

　勢如彍弩節如發機

4 紛紛紜紜鬥亂而不可亂也渾渾沌沌形圓而不可敗也

　亂生于治怯生于勇弱生于強

　治亂數也

勇怯勢也

强弱形也

故善動敵者形之敵必從之予之敵必取之以利動之以卒待之

5 故善戰者求之于勢不貴于人故能擇人而任勢

任勢者其戰人也如轉木石

木石之性安則靜危則動方則止圓則行故善戰人之勢如轉圓石于千仞之山者

勢也

———— ∾∾∾ ————

虛實第六

1 孫子曰

凡先處戰地而待敵者佚後處戰地而趨戰者勞

故善戰者致人而不致于人能使敵人自至者利之也能使敵不得至者害之也

故敵佚能勞之飽能饑之安能動之

2 出其所不趨趨其所不意

行千裏而不勞者行于無人之地也

攻而必取者攻其所不守也

守而必固者守其所不攻也

故善攻者敵不知其所守善守者敵不知其所攻

微乎微乎至于無形神乎神乎至于無聲故能爲敵之司命

3 進而不可禦者衝其虛也退而不可追者速而不可及也

故我欲戰敵雖高壘深溝不得不與我戰者攻其所必救也

我不欲戰劃地而守之敵不得與我戰者乖其所之也

4 故形人而我無形則我專而敵分我專爲一敵分爲十是以十攻其一也
則我衆而敵寡能以衆擊寡者則吾之所與戰者約矣

吾所與戰之地不可知不可知則敵所備者多敵所備者多則吾所
與戰者寡矣

故備前則後寡備後則前寡備左則右寡備右則左寡無所不備則
無所不寡

寡者備人者也衆者使人備己者也

故知戰之地知戰之日則可千裏而會戰

不知戰地不知戰日則左不能救右右不能救左前不能救後後不
能救前而況遠者數十裏近者數裏乎

5 以吾度之越人之兵雖多亦奚益于勝哉故曰勝可爲也

敵雖衆可使無鬥

故策之而知得失之計作之而知動靜之理形之而知死生之地角
之而知有餘不足之處

6 故形兵之極至于無形無形則深間不能窺智者不能謀

因形而措勝于衆衆不能知人皆知我所以勝之形而莫知吾所以
制勝之形

故其戰勝不復而應形於無窮

7 夫兵形象水水之形避高而趨下兵之形避實而擊虛

水因地而制流兵因敵而制勝故兵無常勢水無常形

能因敵變化而取勝者謂之神

故五行無常勝四時無常位日有短長月有死生

217

軍爭第七

1 孫子曰

凡用兵之法將受命於君合軍聚衆交和而捨

莫難於軍爭軍爭之難者以迂爲直以患爲利

故迂其途而誘之以利後人發先人至此知迂直之計者也

2 故軍爭爲利軍爭爲危

舉軍而爭利則不及委軍而爭利則輜重捐

是故卷甲而趨日夜不處倍道兼行百裏而爭利則擒三將軍勁者
先疲者後其法十一而至

五十裏而爭利則蹶上將軍其法半至

三十裏而爭利則三分之二至

是故軍無輜重則亡無糧食則亡無委積則亡

3 故不知諸侯之謀者不能豫交不知山林險阻沮澤之形者不能行軍不
用鄉導者不能得地利

故兵以詐立以利動以分合爲變者也

故其疾如風其徐如林侵掠如火不動如山難知如陰動如雷霆

掠鄉分衆廓地分利

懸權而動

先知迂直之計者勝

此軍爭之法也

4 軍政曰

言不相聞故爲金鼓視不相見故爲旌旗
夫金鼓旌旗者所以一人之耳目也

人既專一則勇者不得獨進怯者不得獨退此用眾之法也

故夜戰多火鼓晝戰多旌旗所以變人之耳目也

5 故三軍可奪氣將軍可奪心

是故朝氣銳晝氣惰暮氣歸

故善用兵者避其銳氣擊其惰歸此治氣者也

以治待亂以靜待譁此治心者也

以近待遠以佚待勞以飽待饑此治力者也

無邀正正之旗勿擊堂堂之陣此治變者也

6 故用兵之法高陵勿向背邱勿逆佯北勿從銳卒勿攻餌兵勿食歸師勿
遏圍師必闕窮寇勿迫

此用兵之法也

———— ∞ ————

九變第八

1 孫子曰

凡用兵之法將受命於君合軍聚眾

2 圯地無舍衢地合交絕地無留圍地則謀死地則戰

塗有所不由軍有所不擊城有所不攻地有所不爭

君命有所不受

3 故將通于九變之利者知用兵矣將不通于九變之利者雖知地形不能
得地之利矣

治兵不知九變之術雖知五利不能得人之用矣

是故智者之慮必雜于利害雜于利而務可信也雜于害而患可解也

4 是故屈諸侯者以害役諸侯者以業趨諸侯者以利

219

故用兵之法無恃其不來恃吾有以待也無恃其不攻恃吾有所不
可攻也

5 故將有五危必死可殺也必生可虜也忿速可侮也廉潔可辱也愛民可
煩也

凡此五者將之過也用兵之災也覆軍殺將必以五危

不可不察也

———— ∞ ————

行軍第九

1 孫子曰

凡處軍相敵

絕山依谷視生處高戰隆無登此處山之軍也

絕水必遠水客絕水而來勿迎之于水內令半濟而擊之利欲戰者
無附于水而迎客視生處高無迎水流此處水上之軍也

絕斥澤惟亟去勿留若交軍于斥澤之中必依水草而背衆樹此處
斥澤之軍也

平陸處易而右背高前死後生此處平陸之軍也

凡此四軍之利黃帝之所以勝四帝也

凡軍好高而惡下貴陽而賤陰養生而處實軍無百疾是謂必勝

邱陵隄防必處其陽而右背之

此兵之利地之助也

2 上雨水沫至欲涉者待其定也

凡地有絕澗天井天牢天羅天陷天隙必亟去之勿近也吾遠之敵
近之吾迎之敵背之

軍行有險阻潢井葭葦山林翳薈者必謹覆索之此伏奸之所也

220

3 敵近而靜者恃其險也遠而挑戰者欲人之進也其所居易者利也
衆樹動者來也衆草多障者疑也

鳥起者伏也獸駭者覆也

塵高而銳者車來也卑而廣者徒來也散而條達者樵採也少而往
來者營軍也

辭卑而益備者進也辭強而進驅者退也

輕車先出居其側者陣也

無約而請和者謀也奔走而陳兵者期也半進半退者誘也

4 仗而立者饑也汲而先飲者渴也

見利而不進者勞也

鳥集者虛也

夜呼者恐也

軍擾者將不重也旌旗動者亂也吏怒者倦也

殺馬肉食軍無懸缶不返其舍者窮寇也

諄諄翕翕涂與人言者失衆也數賞者窘也數罰者困也先暴而後
畏其衆者不精之至也

來委謝者欲休息也

兵怒而相迎久而不合又不相去必謹察之

5 兵非貴益多惟無武進足以併力料敵取人而已

夫惟無慮而易敵者必擒于人

6 卒未親附而罰之則不服不服則難用也卒已親附而罰不行則不可
用也

故令之以文齊之以武是謂必取

令素行以教其民則民服令不素行以教其民則民不服
令素行者與衆相得也

———— ∿∿∿ ————

地形第十

1 孫子曰

地形有通者有挂者有支者有隘者有險者有遠者

我可以注彼可以來曰通通形者先居高陽利糧道以戰則利

可以往難以返曰挂挂形者敵無備出而勝之敵若有備出而不勝
難以返不利

我出而不利彼出而不利曰支支形者敵雖利我我無出也引而去
之令敵半出而擊之利

隘形者我先居之必盈以待敵若敵先居之盈而勿從不盈而從之

險形者我先居之必居高陽以待敵若敵先居之引而去之勿從也

遠形者勢均難以挑戰戰而不利

凡此六者地之道也將之至任不可不察也

2 故兵有走者有弛者有陷者有崩者有亂者有北者

凡此六者非天地之災將之過也

夫勢均以一擊十曰走

卒强吏弱曰弛

吏强卒弱曰陷

大吏怒而不服遇敵懟而自戰將不知其能曰崩

將弱不嚴教道不明吏卒無常陳兵縱橫曰亂

將不能料敵以少合衆以弱擊强兵無選鋒曰北

222

凡此六者敗之道也將之至任不可不察也

3 夫地形者兵之助也料敵制勝計險阨遠近上將之道也

知此而用戰者必勝不知此而用戰者必敗

4 故戰道必勝主曰無戰必戰可也戰道不勝主曰必戰無戰可也

故進不求名退不避罪唯民是保而利合于主國之寶也

視卒如嬰兒故可與之赴深谿視卒如愛子故可與之俱死

厚而不能使愛而不能令亂而不能治譬若驕子不可用也

5 知吾卒之可以擊而不知敵之不可擊勝之半也

知敵之可擊而不知吾卒之不可以擊勝之半也

知敵之可擊知吾卒之可以擊而不知地形之不可以戰勝之半也

故知兵者動而不迷舉而不窮

故曰知彼知己勝乃不殆知天知地勝乃可全

───── ∾∾∾ ─────

九地第十一

1 孫子曰

用兵之法有散地有輕地有爭地有交地有衢地有重地有圮地有
圍地有死地

諸侯自戰其地者為散地

入人之地而不深者為輕地

我得則利彼得亦利者為爭地

我可以往彼可以來者為交地

諸侯之地三屬先至而得天下之眾者為衢地

223

入人之地深背城邑多者爲重地

山林險阻沮澤凡難行之道者爲圮地

所由入者隘所從歸者迂彼寡可以擊吾之衆者爲圍地

疾戰則存不疾戰則亡者爲死地

是故散地則無戰輕地則無止爭地則無攻交地則無絕衢地則合
交重地則掠圮地則行圍地則謀死地則戰

2 古之所謂善用兵者能使敵人前後不相及衆寡不相恃貴賤不相救上
下不相收卒離而不集兵合而不齊

合于利而動不合于利而止

敢問敵衆整而將來待之若何

曰先奪其所愛則聽矣

兵之情主速乘人之不及由不虞之道攻其所不戒也

3 凡爲客之道深入則專主人不克掠于饒野三軍足食

謹養而勿 勞併氣積力運兵計謀爲不可測

投之無所往死且不北死焉不得士人盡力

兵士甚陷則不懼無所往則固深入則拘不得已則鬥

是故其兵不修而戒不求而得不約而親不令而信

禁祥去疑至死無所之

吾士無餘財非惡貨也無餘命非惡壽也

令發之日士卒坐者涕霑襟偃臥者涕交頤投之無所往則諸劌之
勇也

4 故善用兵者譬如率然率然者恆山之蛇也擊其首則尾至擊其尾則首
至擊其中則首尾俱至

敢問兵可使如率然乎曰可

夫吳人與越人相惡也當其同舟而濟遇風其相救也如左右手

是故方馬埋輪未足恃也

齊勇若一政之道也剛柔皆得地之理也

故善用兵者攜手若使一人不得已也

5 將軍之事靜以幽正以治

愚士卒之耳目使之無知

易其事革其謀使人無識

易其居迂其途使人不得慮

帥與之期如登高而去其梯

帥與之深入諸侯之地而發其機

焚舟破釜若驅群羊驅而注驅而來莫知所之

聚三軍之衆投之于險此謂將軍之事也

九地之變屈伸之利人情之理不可不察也

6 凡爲客之道深則專淺則散

去國越境而師者絕地也

四達者衢地也

入深者重地也

入淺者輕地也

背固前隘者圍地也

無所注者死地也

是故散地吾將一其志輕地吾將使之屬爭地吾將趨其後交地吾將謹其守衢地吾將固其結重地吾將繼其食圮地吾將進其途圍地吾將塞其闕死地吾將示之以不活

故兵之情圍則禦不得已則鬥過則從

7 是故不知諸侯之謀者不能預交不知山林險阻沮澤之形者不能行軍不用鄉導者不能得地利

8 四五者不知一非霸王之兵也

夫霸王之兵伐大國則其衆不得聚威加于敵則其交不得合

是故不爭天下之交不養天下之權信己之私威加于敵故其城可拔其國可隳

9 施無法之賞懸無政之令犯三軍之衆若使一人

犯之以事勿告以言犯之以利勿告以害

投之亡地然後存陷之死地然後生

夫衆陷于害然後能爲勝敗

10 故爲兵之事在于順詳敵之意幷敵一向千裏殺將是謂巧能成事者也

11 是故政舉之日夷關折符無通其使

屬于廊廟之上以誅其事

敵人開闔必亟入之先其所愛微與之期

踐墨隨敵以決戰事

是故始如處女敵人開戶後如脫兔敵不及拒

火攻 第十二

1 孫子曰

凡火攻有五一曰火人二曰火積三曰火輜四曰火庫五曰火隊

行火必有因烟火必素具

2 發火有時起火有日時者天之燥也日者月在箕壁翼軫也凡此四宿者
風起之日也

凡火攻必因五火之變而應之

火發于內則早應之于外

火發而其兵靜者待而勿攻極其火力可從而從之不可從而止

火可發于外無待于內以時發之

火發上風無攻下風晝風久夜風止

凡軍必知五火之變以數守之

故以火佐攻者明以水佐攻者強水可以絶不可以奪

3 夫戰勝攻取而不修其攻者凶命曰費留

故曰明主慮之良將修之

非利不動非得不用非危不戰

4 主不可以怒而興師將不可以慍而致戰

合于利而動不合于利而止

怒可以復喜慍可以復悅亡國不可以復存死者不可以復生

故明君慎之良將警之

此安國全軍之道也

用間第十三

1 孫子曰

　　凡興師十萬出征千裏百姓之費公家之奉日費千金内外騷動怠于道路不得操事者七十萬家

　　相守數年以爭一日之勝

　　而愛爵祿百金不知敵之情者不仁之至也非人之將也非主之佐也非勝之主也

　　故明君賢將所以動而勝人成功出于衆者先知也

　　先知者不可取于鬼神不可象于事不可驗于度必取于人知敵之情者也

2 故用間有五有鄉間有内間有反間有死間有生間

　　五間俱起莫知其道是謂神紀人君之寶也

　　鄉間者因其鄉人而用之

　　内間者因其官人而用之

　　反間者因其敵間而用之

　　死間者爲誑事于外令吾間知之而傳于敵間也

　　生間者反報也

3 故三軍之事親莫親于間賞莫厚于間事莫密于間

　　非聖智不能用間非仁義不能使間非微妙不能得間之實

　　微哉微哉無所不用間也間事未發而先聞者間與所告者皆死

4 凡軍之所欲擊城之所欲攻人之所欲殺必先知其守將左右謁者門者舍人之姓名令吾間必索知之

　　必索敵人之間來間我者因而利之導而舍之故反間可得而用也

　　因是而知之故鄉間内間可得而使也因是而知之故死間爲誑事

可使告敵因是而知之故生間可使如期

五間之事主必知之知之必在于反間故反間不可不厚也

昔殷之興也伊摯在夏周之興也呂牙在殷

5 故惟明君賢將能以上智為間者必成大功

此兵之要三軍之所恃而動也

THE SCIENCE OF WAR

BIBLIOGRAPHY

Military and strategic

China's Evolving Military Strategy, edited by Joe McReynolds. The Jamestown Foundation, Washington, DC, 2016.

The Improbable War: China, the United States and the Logic of Great Power Conflict, by Christopher Coker. Hurst & Company, London, 2015.

War: What is it Good For? by Ian Morris. Profile Books, London, 2014.

The Utility of Force: The Art of War in the Modern World, by Rupert Smith. Penguin, London, 2006.

Imagined Enemies: China Prepares for Uncertain War, by John Wilson Lewis and Xue Litai. Stanford University Press, Stanford, 2006.

If China Attacks Taiwan: Military Strategy, Politics and Economics, edited by Steve Tsang. Routledge, Abingdon, 2006.

War of the Flea, by Robert Taber. Potomac Book, Virginia, 2002.

Makers of Modern Strategy: from Machiavelli to the Nuclear Age, edited by Peter Paret. Princeton University Press, 1986.

The Strategy of Conflict, by Thomas C. Schelling. Harvard University Press, Cambridge (Massachusetts), 1980.

Ancient China

Deciphering Sun Tzu: How to Read the Art of War, by Derek M. C. Yuen. Hurst & Company, London, 2014.

The Dao of the Military: Liu An's Art of War, by Andrew Seth Meyer. Columbia University Press, New York, 2012.

THE SCIENCE OF WAR

Sun Tzu on the Art of War, translated by Lionel Giles. Barnes & Noble, New York, 2012.

Ancient Chinese Thought, Modern Chinese Power, by Yan Xuetong. Princeton University Press, Princeton, 2011.

Imperial Warlord: A Biography of Cao Cao, 155-220 AD, by Rafe de Crespigny. Brill, Leiden, 2010.

Ancient China on Postmodern War, by Thomas M. Kane. Routledge, Abingdon, 2007.

Sun Tzu's Art of War: The Modern Chinese Translation, by General Tao Hanzhang. Sterling Publishing Company, New York, 2007

The Art of War: Sun Zi's Military Methods, translated by Victor H. Mair. Columbia University Press, New York, 2007.

Chinese History: A Manual, by Endymion Wilkinson. Harvard University Asia Center, Cambridge (Massachusetts), 2000.

A Short History of Chinese Philosophy, by Fung Yu-lan. The Free Press, New York, 1997.

Sunzi Bingfa: Han-Ying dui zhao, translation by Yuan Shibing. Foreign Language Teaching and Research Press, Beijing,1997

Sunzi shisan pian yuwen duben, by Yao Li-nung. Taiwan Commercial Press, Tapei, 1995

Sun Tzu: Art of War, translated and introduced by Ralph Sawyer. Westview Press, Boulder, 1994

Sun-Tzu: The Art of Warfare, translated by Roger Ames. Ballantine Books, New York, 1993.

The Seven Military Classics of Ancient China, translated and introduced by Ralph Sawyer. Basic Books, New York, 1993.

Sanctioned Violence in Early China, by Mark Edward Lewis. State University of New York Press, Albany, 1990.

The Cambridge History of China Volume 1: The Ch'in and Han Empires 221 B.C. – A.D. 220, edited by Denis Twitchett and Michael Loewe. Cambridge University Press, Cambridge, 1986.

The Chinese Machiavelli: Three Thousand Years of Chinese Statecraft, by Ching Ping and Dennis Bloodworth. Secker and Warburg, London, 1976.

Sun Tzu: The Art of War, translated by Samuel B. Griffith. Oxford University Press, Oxford, 1963.

Contemporary China

The Hundred Year Marathon, by Michael Pillsbury. St. Martin's Griffin, New York, 2015.

Never Forget National Humiliation: Historical Memory in Chinese Politics and Foreign Relations, by Zheng Wang. Columbia University Press, New York, 2012.

On China, by Henry Kissinger. The Penguin Press, New York, 2011.

The Mind of Empire: China's History and Modern Foreign Relations, by Christopher A. Ford. The University Press of Kentucky, 2010.

The Party: The Secret World of China's Communist Rulers, by Richard McGregor. Harper, New York, 2010.

Underground Front: The Chinese Communist Party in Hong Kong, by Christine Loh. Hong Kong University Press, Hong Kong, 2010.

Mao: The Unknown Story, by Jung Chang and Jon Halliday. Jonathan Cape, London, 2005.

Power Shift: China and Asia's New Dynamics, edited by David Shambaugh. University of California Press, Berkeley, 2005.

The Search for Modern China, by Jonathan D. Spence. W. W. Norton & Company, New York, 1990.

Taiwan

Forbidden Nation: A History of Taiwan, by Jonathan Manthorpe. Palgrave Macmillan, New York, 2009.

Political Conflict and Economic Interdependence Across the Taiwan Strait and Beyond, by Scott L. Kastner. Stanford University Press, Stanford, 2009.

How Taiwan Became Chinese: Dutch, Spanish and Han Colonization in the Seventeenth Century, by Tonio Andrade. Columbia University Press, New York, 2008.

Taiwan's Security: History and Prospects, by Bernard D. Cole. Routledge, Abingdon, 2006.

Dangerous Strait: The U.S.-Taiwan-China Crisis, edited by Nancy Bernkopf Tucker. Columbia University Press, New York, 2005.

Is Taiwan Chinese? The Impact of Culture, Power, and Migration on Changing Identities, by Melissa J. Brown. University of California Press, Berkeley, 2004.

Peace and Security Across the Taiwan Strait, edited by Steve Tsang. Palgrave Macmillan, Basingstoke, 2004.

Formosa Betrayed, by George H. Kerr. Eyre & Spottiswoode, London, 1966.

General history

Genghis Khan and the Making of the Modern World, by Jack Weatherford. Three River Press, New York, 2004.

Genghis Khan: Life, death and resurrection, by John Man. Bantam Books, London, 2004.

The Napoleonic Empire, by Geoffrey Ellis. Palgrave Macmillan, Basingstoke, 2003.

Napoleon and the Transformation of Europe, by Alexander Grab. Palgrave Macmillan, Basingstoke, 2003.

Voltaire's Bastards: The dictatorship of reason in the west, by John Ralston Saul, The Free Press, New York, 1992.

Genghis Khan: His Life and Legacy, by Paul Ratchnevsky. Blackwell, Oxford, 1991

Selected online resources
These can be located online by title and/or author.

The Chinese Military: Overview and Issues for Congress, by Ian E. Rinehart. Congressional Research Service, March 2016.

CHRISTOPHER MACDONALD

5 Maps that Explain China's Strategy, by George Friedman. Mauldin Economics courtesy of Business Insider, January 2016.

Cooperation, Competition and Shaping the Outlook: the United States and China's neighbourhood diplomacy, by Wu Xinbo. International Affairs 92, 2016.

Annual Report to Congress: Military and Security Developments Involving the People's Republic of China 2016. Office of the Secretary of Defense, 2016.

China's Evolving Approach to "Integrated Strategic Deterrence", by Michael S. Chase and Arthur Chan. RAND Corporation 2016.

Air Defense Options for Taiwan: An Assessment of Relative Costs and Operational Benefits, by Michael J. Lostumbo et al. RAND Corporation 2016.

War with China: Thinking Through the Unthinkable, by David C. Gompert et al. RAND Corporation 2016.

China's Grand Strategy, by Simon Norton. The University of Sydney China Studies Centre, November 2015.

The Thucydides Trap: Are the U.S. and China Headed for War? by Graham Allison. The Atlantic, September 2015.

Chinese Views, Strategy and Geopolitics, by Robert Kaplan. John Hopkins University Applied Physics Laboratory "Rethinking Seminar Series", January 2015.

China's Incomplete Military Transformation: Assessing the Weaknesses of the People's Liberation Army (PLA), by Michael S. Chase et al. RAND Corporation 2015.

The U.S.-China Military Scorecard: Forces, Geography and the Evolving Balance of Power 1996-2017, by Eric Heginbotham et al. RAND Corporation 2015.

Chinese Strategy and Military Power in 2014: Chinese, Japanese, Korean, Taiwanese and US Perspectives, by Anthony H. Cordesman. Center for Strategic & International Studies (CSIS), November 2014.

Understanding China's Political System, by Susan V. Lawrence and Michael F. Martin. Congressional Research Service, March 2013.

China: The Three Warfares, prepared by Prof. Stefan Halper. Office of the Secretary of Defense, 2013.

Old – But Strong – Wine in New Bottles: China's "Three Warfares", by Prof. James R. Holmes. In China: The Three Warfares, Stefan Halper, Office of the Secretary of Defense, 2013.

China at the Crossroads, by Francis Godemont. European Council on Foreign Relations, April 2012.

China's Search for a Grand Strategy: a rising power finds its way, by Wang Jisi. Foreign Affairs, March 2011.

General Liu Yuan's Preface to Zhang Musheng's 'Changing Our View of Culture and History', in translation. Delex Systems, September 2011.

Anti-Access/Area Denial: The Evolution of Modern Warfare, by Major Christopher J. McCarthy. Naval War College, 2010.

China and the Principle of Self-Determination of Peoples, by anonymous. St Antony's International Review 6, 2010.

Peaceful Rise through Unrestricted Warfare: Grand Strategy with Chinese Characteristics, by Tony Corn. Small Wars Journal, 2010.

Chinese Economic Coercion Against Taiwan: A Tricky Weapon to Use, by Murray Scot Tanner. RAND Corporation, 2007.

Chinese Text Project: Pre-Qin and Han. ctext-org, 2006-2007.

China's 'Peaceful Rise': Concept and Practice, by Yongnian Zheng and Sow Keat Tok. University of Nottingham China Policy Institute, November 2005.

One-China Policy and Taiwan, by Y. Frank Chiang. Fordham International Law Journal 28:1, 2004.

Chinese Military-related Think Tanks and Research Institutions, by Bates Gill and James Mulvenon. China Quarterly, September 2002.

Interpreting China's Grand Strategy: Past, Present and Future, by Michael D. Swaine and Ashley J. Tellis. RAND Corporation 2000.

Sonshi.com: Educational resource for Sun Tzu's The Art of War. Since 1999.

Sun Tzu and Clausewitz: The Art of War and On War Compared, by Michael Handel. US Army War College Strategic Studies Institute, 1991.

Unrestricted Warfare by Qiaoliang and Wang Xiangshui, translated by Foreign Broadcast Information Service (FBIS). Courtesy of crytome.org, undated.

THE SCIENCE OF WAR

238

INDEX

infantry, 26; media, 114; "modern", 82; new system/form of, 15, 68; perpetual, 46; philosophical treatises on, 22; political, 114; principles of, 30, 83; psychological, 114; regimented model of, 14; spiral of, 84; thirteen-part treatise on, 9; transition in, 11

warlord(s), 50-51, 56

warplane(s), 111

Warring State(s), 42, 90, 104, 119, 121 army, 29; era, 32, 41, 45, 80, 99; lens, 86; paradigm, 85-86, 104, 122; texts, 20; transition, 15, 20, 27; treatises, 107; vision of the future, 90; world, 41

Warring States period, the (5th century BC to 221 BC), 14-15, 18, 20, 22, 24, 44-45, 83

Washington, D. C., 112

Waterloo, battle of (1815), 76

weapons and weaponry, 19, 25, 28, 79, 108 bronze, 11; defensive, 110; wood and stone, 11

weather conditions, 40

Wei, kingdom of, 18-19

Wei River, 54

Wellington, Duke of (1769-1852), 76

Western Pacific, 98

Western world, 92

wet-rice farming, 8

White Wolf Mountain, battle of (AD 207), 54

woodblock editions, 66

world-under-heaven (*tianxia*), 45, 86, 95, 119

World Bank, 88

World War I (1914-1918), 79-80

World War II (1939-1945), 80, 93, 101, 105

WTO (World Trade Organization), 112

Wu Qi (440-381 BC), 22

Wu, kingdom of, 4-8, 20, 94 annexed by Yue, 21; conflict with Chu, 12; invasion and conquest of Chu, 13, 49; peripheral and fast-rising, 12; zenith of power, 15

Wuhuan confederation, 54

Wuzi, the, 22

Xinjiang, 89

xu-shi (虛實) (the empty and the solid), 34-35

Yangtze River, 5 regions of the South, 14;

Yellow River, 5, 51, 54, 60 plain 33; states, 14

Yellow Sea, 95

Yelü Chucai, 67

Yinchuan, Tangut capital, 59

Ying, capital of Chu, 9

Yin-yang

ABOUT THE AUTHOR

Christopher MacDonald is a translator and interpreter based in Cardiff. He spent a year in Xian in 1985, and has since lived and worked in Taipei, Hong Kong and Shanghai as a translator, interpreter and trade and investment consultant. From 1997 to 1999 he was the interpreter for the British side in the Sino-British Joint Liaison Group. *The Science of War* is his first book.